CW00401008

The ART of Life Drawing

The ART of Life Drawing

Jane Stanton

ARTISTS HOUSE

Edited and designed by the Artists House Division
of Mitchell Beazley International Ltd
Artists House, 14-15 Manette Street, London W1V 5LB

Design: Hans Verkroost
Editor: Alexandra Russell
Production: Peter Phillips
Stewart Bowling

ISBN 0 86134 119 8

Typeset by Hourds Typographica, Stafford
Origination by La Cromolito s.n.c., Milan
Printed in Portugal by Printer Portuguesa Graphica Lda.

CONTENTS

INTRODUCTION

Since our terms of reference come from our own experiences, it is not surprising that the largest proportion of visual imagery of the last two thousand years has concerned the human figure. Apart from being the most familiar subject that we can draw, figures also give a sense of scale and proportion to an image, even if they are only incidental to the scene portrayed.

Drawing is the most immediate way of capturing or studying a subject. It is a useful skill to learn whether you end up drawing the figure or something else.

In this book I have adopted what I feel is a realistic approach to figure drawing. In other words, this is *not* intended to be an artist's manual for drawing the figure with biological accuracy.

Figure drawing focuses on the human form, of course, and relies on a reasonably thorough understanding of anatomy. So I've included a basic and simple survey of what I believe to be the essential elements. However, it is my opinion that if you look hard enough at your model, you will see quite clearly how the muscles and the skeleton shape the figure. I also believe that no matter how much anatomy theory we learn, it cannot tell us everything because every person is different in size and proportion from the next. In the end, successful figure drawing depends on careful observation, concentration and practice.

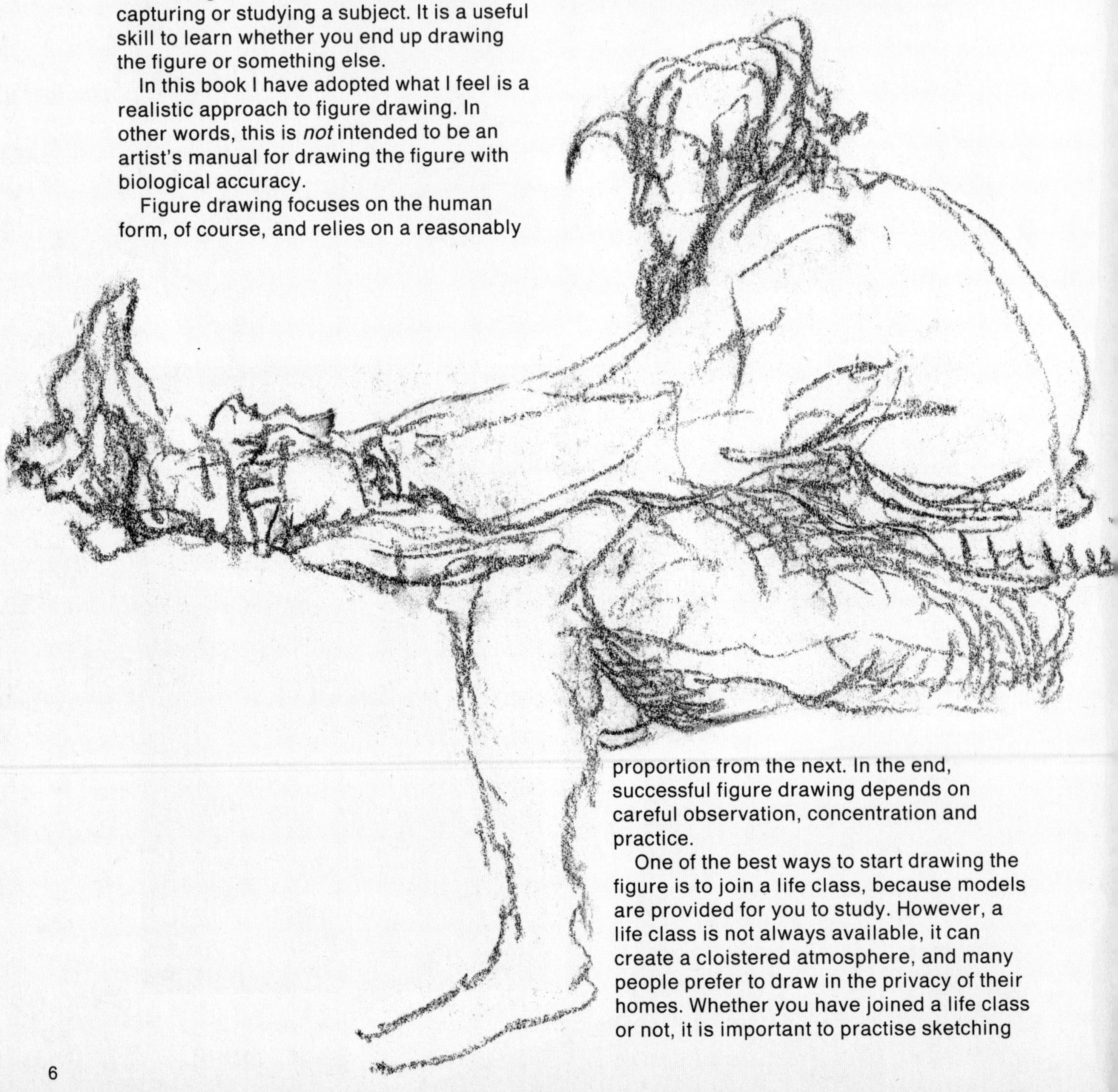

One of the best ways to start drawing the figure is to join a life class, because models are provided for you to study. However, a life class is not always available, it can create a cloistered atmosphere, and many people prefer to draw in the privacy of their homes. Whether you have joined a life class or not, it is important to practise sketching

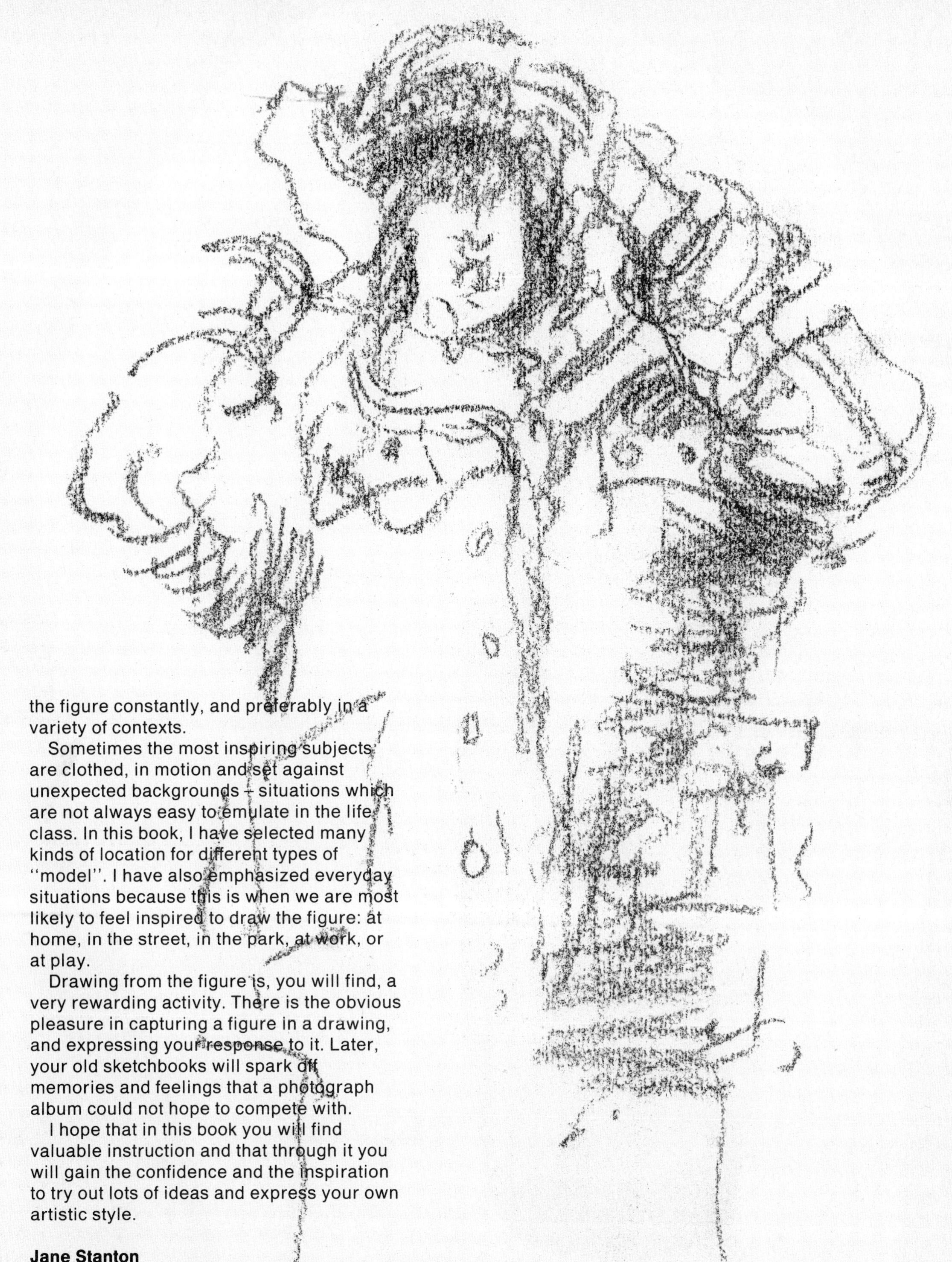

the figure constantly, and preferably in a variety of contexts.

Sometimes the most inspiring subjects are clothed, in motion and set against unexpected backgrounds – situations which are not always easy to emulate in the life class. In this book, I have selected many kinds of location for different types of "model". I have also emphasized everyday situations because this is when we are most likely to feel inspired to draw the figure: at home, in the street, in the park, at work, or at play.

Drawing from the figure is, you will find, a very rewarding activity. There is the obvious pleasure in capturing a figure in a drawing, and expressing your response to it. Later, your old sketchbooks will spark off memories and feelings that a photograph album could not hope to compete with.

I hope that in this book you will find valuable instruction and that through it you will gain the confidence and the inspiration to try out lots of ideas and express your own artistic style.

Jane Stanton

HISTORY

Right: some of the earliest representations of the human figure are these engravings on a limestone cave wall near Palermo, in Sicily. They date from the 7th millennium BC.

Below right: a Greek brush drawing on a ceramic oil flask, c.460–430BC. This drawing, which shows a woman helping a warrior to arm himself, demonstrates an economical and elegant use of line. It is very sophisticated in comparison to the cave painting shown above.

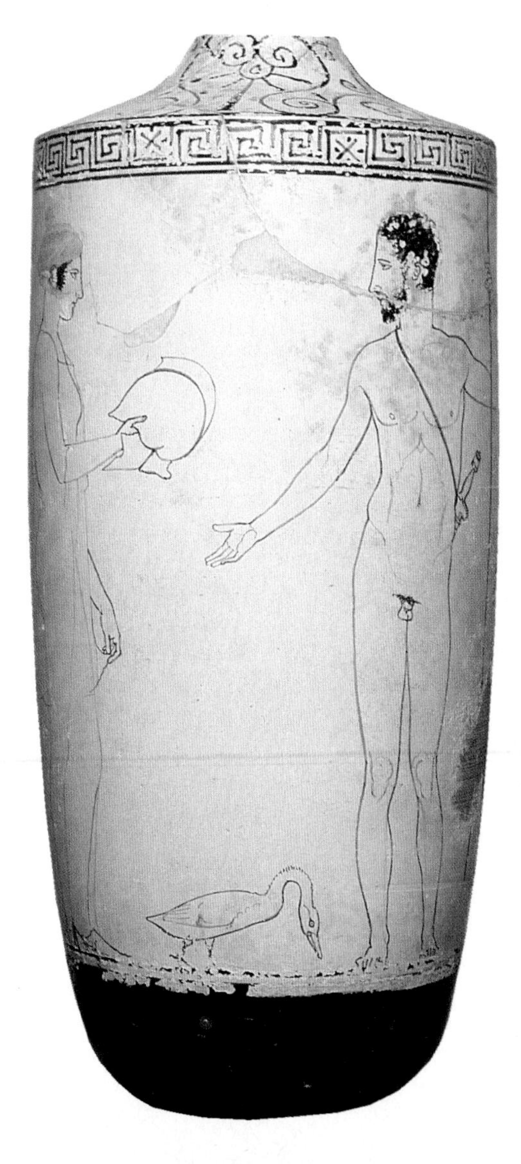

No matter how small a figure is in a picture, it will eventually attract the interest of the spectator. This is because the human form is the most familiar image and something a person can relate to immediately.

Man has been obsessed with images of himself since the earliest times, when he depicted himself hunting in the wild, on cave walls and rock surfaces. But this representation of the human figure was usually stylized and served a symbolic purpose. It was not until the Greek Classical Period, in the fifth century BC, that the body was considered to be an object of beauty in its own right.

It was the Greeks who made the first realistic representations of the human figure, although even then it was idealized. All that remains of these images is in the form of sculpture, ceramic decoration and wall painting, but they still have a strong influence on art today.

Classical concepts of proportions and physical perfection went on to influence Roman art, but died with the Roman Empire. They were not revived until the fourteenth and fifteenth centuries, in the Renaissance, which was literally the rebirth of classical views.

During the Renaissance, life drawings came into their own, when they were done as studies for larger, commissioned oil paintings. Huge studios, which employed full-time models to sit for these studies, were run by the great artists to produce the commissioned works. Artists such as Rubens, Michelangelo, Leonardo and Raphael all came from this tradition. The studies were usually drawn in red chalk and then pricked with pins so that chalk could be pounced through the holes onto the support. The pin pricks perforating the outlines of these studies can still be seen.

It was not until Rembrandt's time, in the seventeenth century, that drawing from life took on a tender and more domestic character, in sharp contrast to the bravura and grandeur of the great Italian masters. Many of Rembrandt's drawings, for example, were done for their own sake, depicting his wife, his son, peasants and beggars, and other types of quite ordinary people. He usually worked on a small scale, using pen and ink or brush and wash. Like the works of the Italian masters, these drawings were the result of an intensive, academic study of anatomy.

Arguably the greatest painters of the female nude were those of nineteenth-century France. Ingres, for example, was probably the most perfect draughtsman of his age. His technical ability was astounding, and he insisted on

Above: *The Three Graces* by Raphael (1483–1520) is a beautifully rhythmical drawing in red chalk, in which the female form has been carefully observed and modelled.

Right: The informality of this pen (or quill) and ink drawing of a peasant woman, by Rembrandt (1606–69), is in stark contrast to Raphael's drawing above. It is more down-to-earth and has a boldness of touch.

absolute precision.

This attention to detail meant that after Ingres French painting became very academic and mannered. Towards the end of the century artists were reacting against this rigidity. Painters such as Manet and his school rejected the falseness of the studio environment. They drew and painted in the open air, using the effects of natural light to give volume and shape to figures instead of relying on cross-hatching to mould form. This was the beginning of Impressionism.

The movement was a great liberator for artists. Now any subject was considered worthy enough to make a drawing or painting from. Absolute and slavish accuracy gave way to sensation and spirit. In addition, the invention of the camera helped artists to realize novel viewpoints and "cut-off" compositions that were quite dramatic.

Degas, who was a great exponent of Impressionism, took many photographs to help in his work. His concern with the unglamorous realities of life is reflected in his famous pastel

drawings of dancers, which are very down-to-earth and evocative of the tough life a dancer leads.

Vincent van Gogh was influenced by Impressionism, even though he was a great individualist and self-taught. His conté crayon drawings of the miners in Belgium and the rough and passionate sketches of friends, neighbours and family, represent a deep feeling for his fellow man and an almost complete lack of adherence to the traditional exactness that Ingres had insisted on.

Bridging the nineteenth and twentieth centuries was a group of young painters who called themselves *Les Fauves* ("the savages"), one of the most famous members of which was Matisse. These artists virtually abandoned perspective, natural colour and natural light for primitive art. However, they were all (and this goes too for the more abstract artists who

Right: this crayon and wash drawing of two peasant girls working in the fields was drawn by Pissarro (1831–1903). It is simple, direct and full of life, and was obviously made on location.

Below: Degas (1834–1917) drew this pastel study of a girl in a tub as part of a series of drawings of girls washing and drying themselves.

followed) schooled in the old academic life-drawing methods, and were superb draughtsmen.

With the onset of "experimental art" and total abstraction in the twentieth century, the need for any kind of exercise in life drawing was questioned. By the 1950s it was considered to be irrelevant to art. Thankfully, though moderation prevailed and, as seems to be true of all phases in the history of art, this idea is now unfashionable. Life classes are once again considered to be the foundation of an artist's career.

Left: this flowing drawing of the Holy Family, by Tiepolo (1696–1770) was probably a study for a painting, and was done in pen with a sepia wash. The scene was probably posed with a real baby.

Below: the English artist Gwen John (1876–1939) made this tender study of a young girl in charcoal and wash in 1918. The model is rather stiffly posed, but this serves to accentuate the awkwardness of youth and perhaps indicate a rather shy character.

Below: *La Collation* (or The Snack) was drawn by the Impressionist painter Renoir (1841–1919). It is a pretty drawing, done in red conté crayon, and shows an intimately observed scene of three women chatting and settling down for a light meal.

ANATOMY AND THE BASIC RULES

This section deals with the more academic aspects of life drawing. It describes the basic elements of anatomy that are useful for an artist to know, and some of the basic tenets of making a picture.

However, there is no need, I feel, to get too bogged down in the very involved subject of human anatomy, because if you look carefully enough when you draw, you will see the forms underneath the skin. What I intend to do is point out some basic rules and truths that are useful to follow when you begin life drawing. These will become second nature after a few years of experience and practice.

I have also described here the rules of composition, lighting and tone. They, too, are complex, but it is important to absorb and practise them before you try to concentrate on drawing. This is how all the great artists have worked.

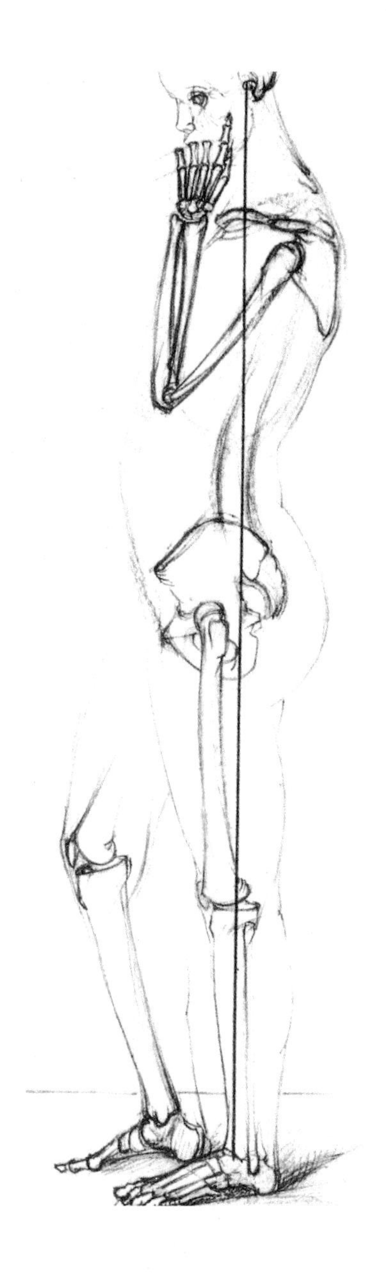

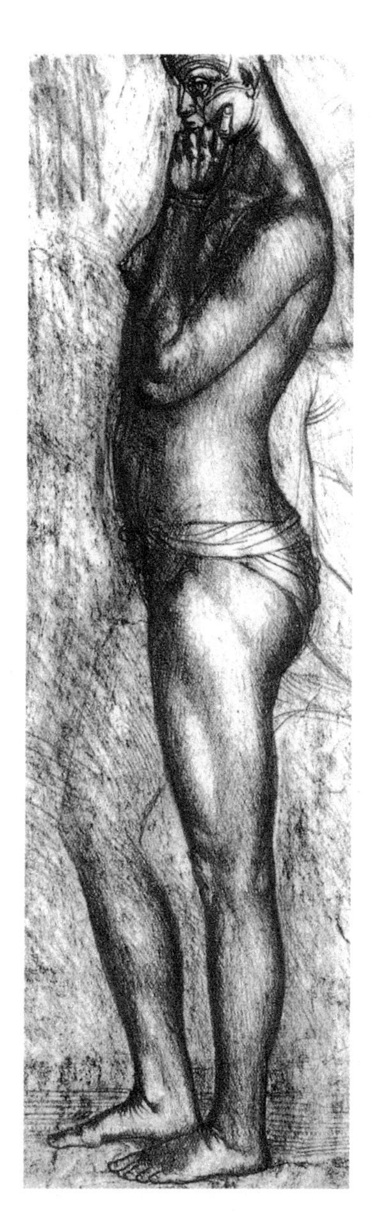

BASIC STUDIO EQUIPMENT

When you are starting to draw for the first time, use a limited amount of equipment. There is so much to choose from that, if you are not selective, it will be too much to cope with and your aims will become confused.

If you are attending a well-run life class, it may have all the necessary equipment available. This will include an artist's donkey, which you can sit astride, or an easel, which you can work at either standing or sitting. However, if you are at home, you can do just as well using a drawing board on a table or balanced on your knee.

If you are going to draw at home, choose a well-lit room with plenty of space, so that you can position yourself at a reasonable distance away from the model. A comfortable chair is also essential, as you may spend hours motionless in one position.

I suggest that you start off with pencil, charcoal or conté crayons, a large stick of fairly cheap cartridge/drawing paper, and an A1 size ($23\frac{3}{8} \times 33\frac{1}{8}$in) drawing board made of wood or plastic and some tape or clips. It is a good idea to have a wastepaper bin close at hand in which you can discard "mistakes" as well as pencil shavings, so that your model does not get his or her feet dirty.

It may sound obvious, but it is a good idea to wear old clothes, or a smock over your ordinary clothes. Drawing can be just as messy as painting, and it is best not to be inhibited in any way before you start.

FINDING AND SETTING UP A MODEL

The best way to find a model is to join a class where all the organizing is done for you. If this is not possible, you can always call an art school and ask them if they could let you have a list of models.

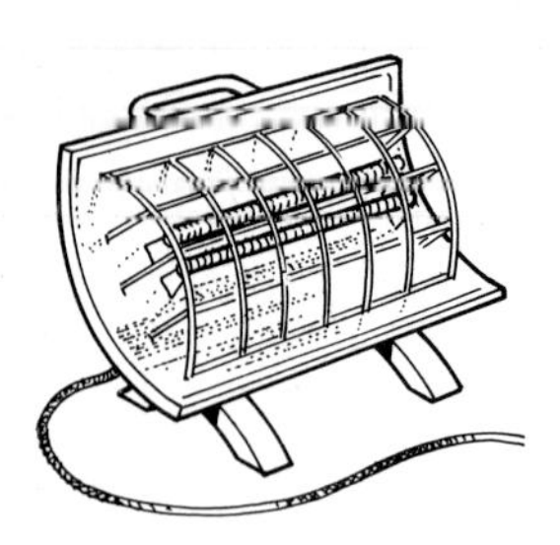

Above: some kind of portable source of heat is vital in a studio. An electric heater is particularly suitable, and safe. A chaise longue, **far right**, is a good compromise between a sofa, a bed, and a chair.

Always remember beforehand whether or not the model will be posing clothed or unclothed. Models often like a separate room, or at least a screen, where they can undress in private. Also check, if you are having more than one model posing together, that they are aware of this. Some may object.

The model's comfort should be uppermost in your considerations. If it is, your model is likely to be cooperative and you will probably get some excellent work out of the session. If your model is cold or in an uncomfortable position, you will run into problems and disagreements.

Make sure that the room is warm enough, especially if the model is nude. Remember, it is

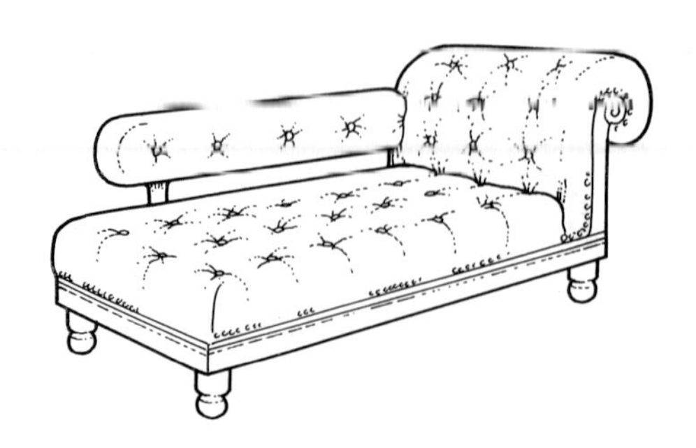

Below: in a life class there should be lots of space and a source of natural as well as artificial light, plus a screen for the model to change behind.

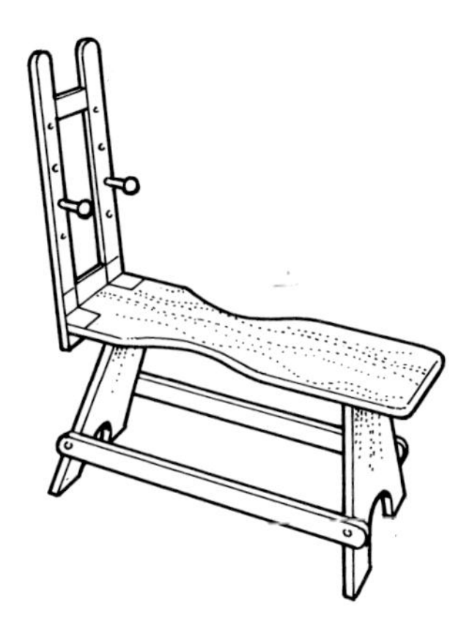

Above and right: the artist's donkey and the easel are two of the most essential pieces of furniture in a life class. You can work sitting down at the one, and standing up at the other.

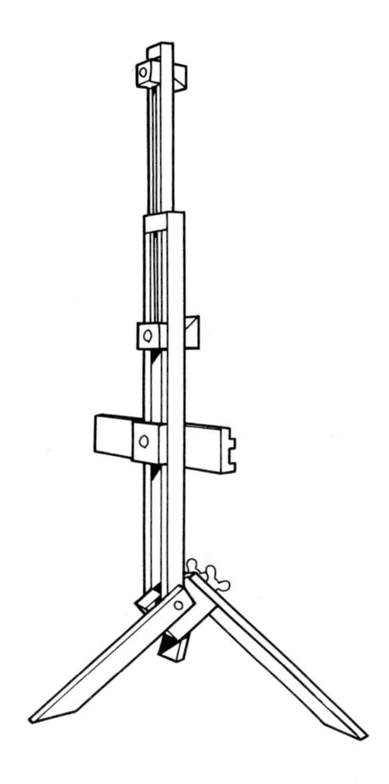

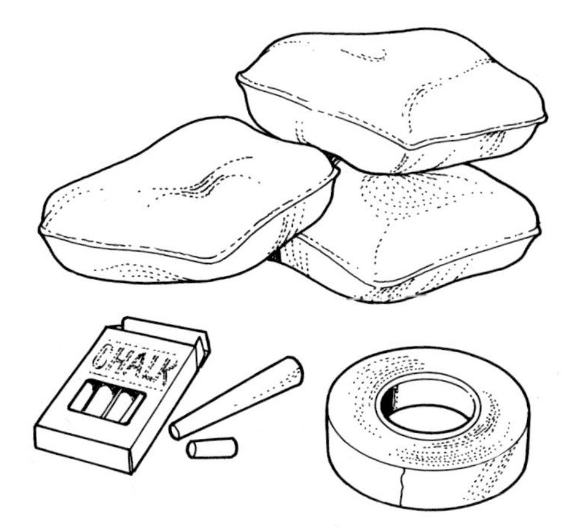

Above and below: other important elements in a studio are chalk or tape, to mark the model's position; cushions on which to support the model; blankets for warmth or decoration; a waste bin to keep the place tidy; and plants and a mirror for added interest in composition.

all right for you because you have your clothes on! You will need at least two electric heaters to be available.

Establish with your model when his or her breaks are due. Some models will pose for an hour or more in a comfortable position, whereas others need a break every thirty minutes. I always let them have a "shake out" every half-hour, and a break for a hot drink after an hour-and-a-half.

Try to get the model to pose in a natural way. I personally would avoid old-fashioned, "heroic" poses – they look false and are also very difficult to hold for any length of time. Remember that a standing position is the most tiring. A reclining pose would be better for a sitting extended over several days.

As props, it is useful to have some interesting chairs around, and perhaps a bed or a sofa with a generous supply of blankets and cushions which you can arrange underneath and around your model. Experiment with different lighting effects, by using spotlights and blacking out the natural light. A collection of brightly coloured and patterned lengths of cloth, and large potted plants, can also add interest to your compositions.

Lastly, a piece of chalk is vital, to mark your model's position when he or she moves for a break.

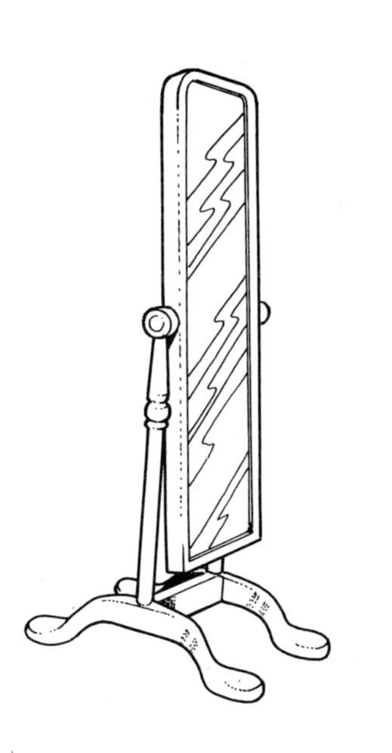

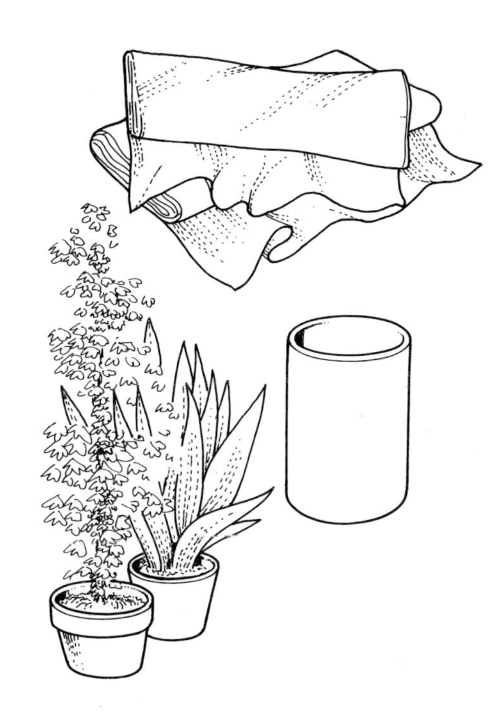

THE SKELETON

The skeleton is the chassis of the human body. It provides a basic rigid structure to protect and support the body to move in an incredible variety of ways. To appreciate fully the importance of the skeleton in shaping the human form you should study it carefully.

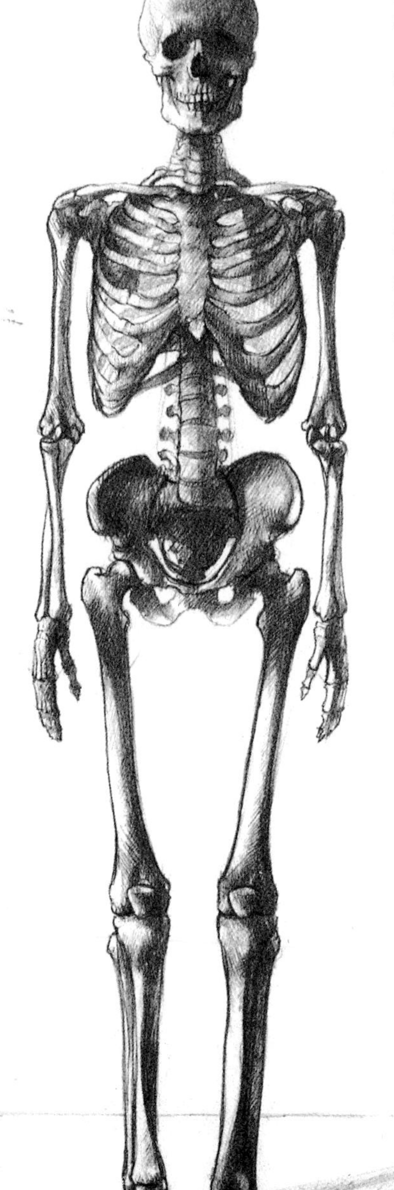

The places on the body where you would expect to notice the skeleton are the knees, hands, elbows, shoulders (the collar bone particularly), the head and the pelvic region (the hip bones) – anywhere, in fact, where the joints of the skeleton allow movement.

The largest masses of bone are found in the skull, the rib cage and the pelvis. These protect the most vital organs of the body and are linked together by the spine.

The spinal column is a remarkable structure made up of alternating rings of cartilage and bone. Barely visible when you are drawing from the model, it is the most important part of the skeleton to understand because it gives the body its flexibility and, at the same time, limits the movements of its various parts.

Left and right: try to draw a skeleton at least once, just to get an idea of the rigid structure underneath the skin. The basic shape of the front and rear view is similar, but you will notice that the pelvic bone and shoulder blades come forward in the rear view. You can also properly appreciate the range of movement allowed in the spinal region between the pelvis and the rib cage where there is very little bone mass to hinder flexibility.

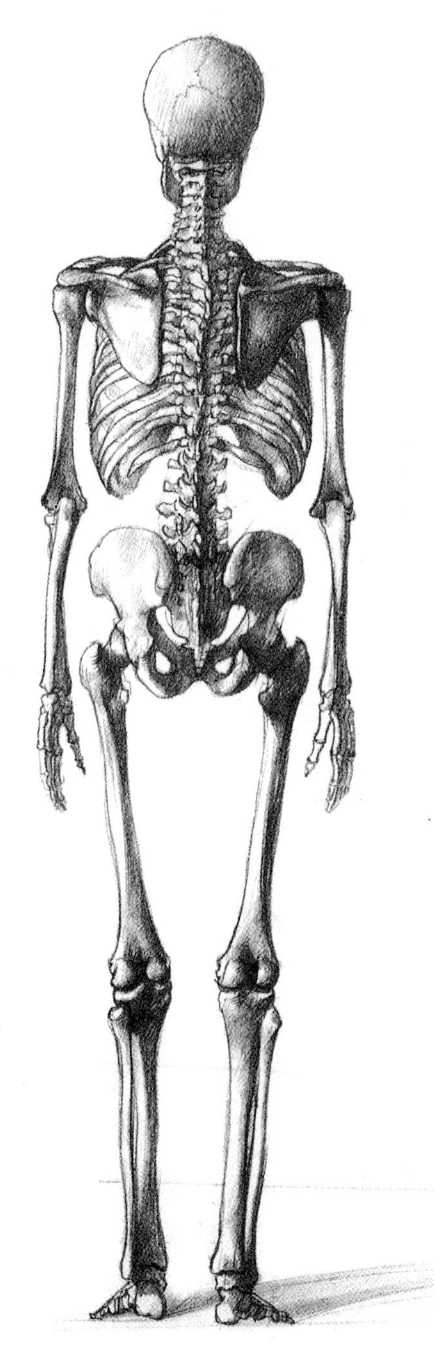

Right: this drawing shows how the bones of the arm are linked to the shoulder blade; the drawing, **far right**, demonstrates how the bones of the leg join the pelvis. The ball-and-socket joint of the shoulder and hip, and the hinge joints of the knees and elbows, allow a remarkable variety of movements.

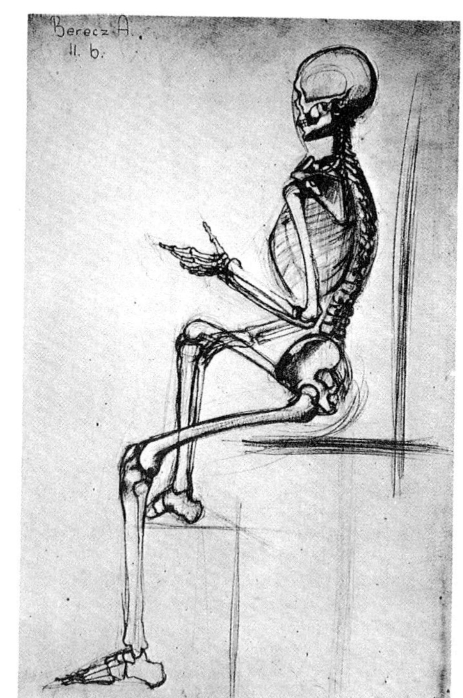

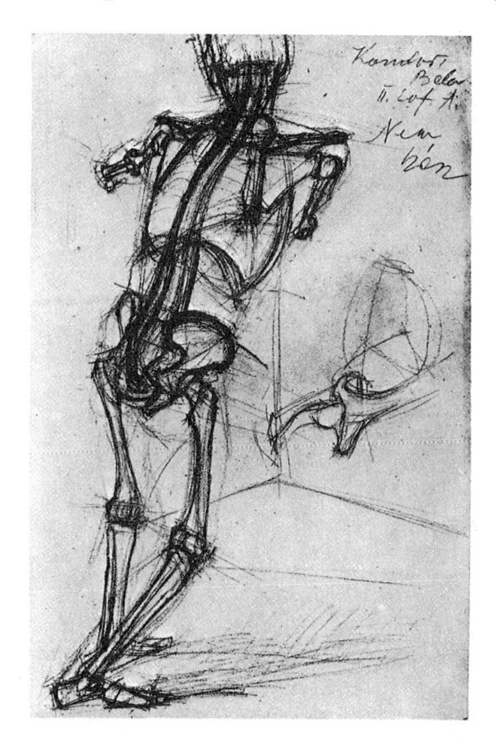

Above and left: it is useful to practise drawing little diagrams which show how the skeleton moves, in order to understand how the joints operate.

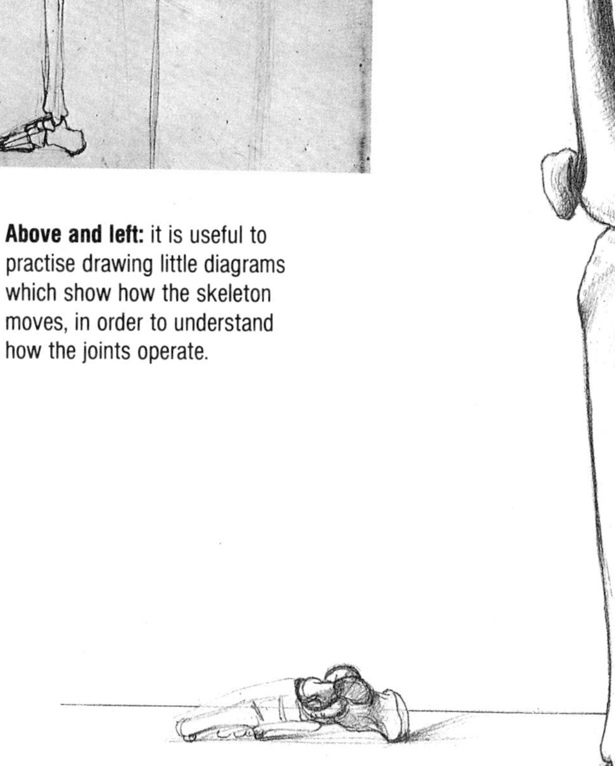

MUSCLES

It is useful for an artist to know where all the muscles are in the body because, together with the skeleton, they give its different parts their shape. Muscles also enable the parts of the skeleton to move.

Muscles work in groups in order to allow a variety of movements. For example, as some contract, others relax and vice versa (these are called anatagonistic muscles). Some are very large, as in the *latissimus dors*, in the back. This is a broad flat muscle. Others are very small, such as the *corrugator* in the head, which helps to draw the eyebrows together.

Proper study of muscular structure as shown in anatomy books is rewarding, but even these books will not tell you all you need to know. If you compare a boxer's or bodybuilder's figure with that of a Sumo wrestler or a presidential candidate, for example, you will find that there is very much more variation in the human body than textbooks indicate.

In addition, people's muscles develop in different ways, according to the kind of physical work they do. Age and sex also affect the appearance of muscles. In a woman's body and in a child's, for example, you will often find it quite hard to distinguish any muscles at all.

As you study a person, you will notice that their muscles alter their shape, size and visibility on the surface depending on the figure's pose. Again, I do emphasize that there is no substitute for very careful observation of your model because every figure is different.

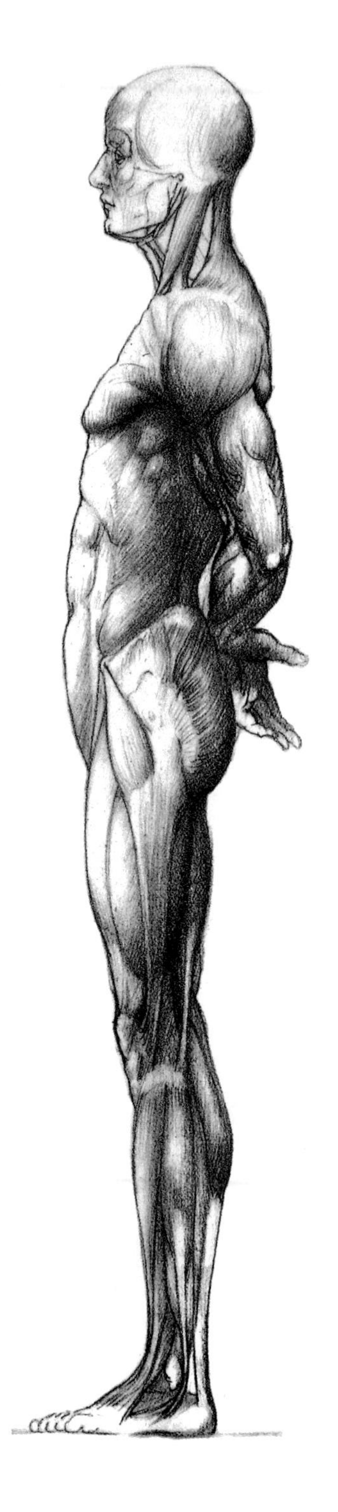

Left and right: the muscular structure of the human body is complex, as these drawings show. The diagram on the left illustrates how the muscles cover the bone structure, and the view on the right displays the pattern and variety of the muscle groups.

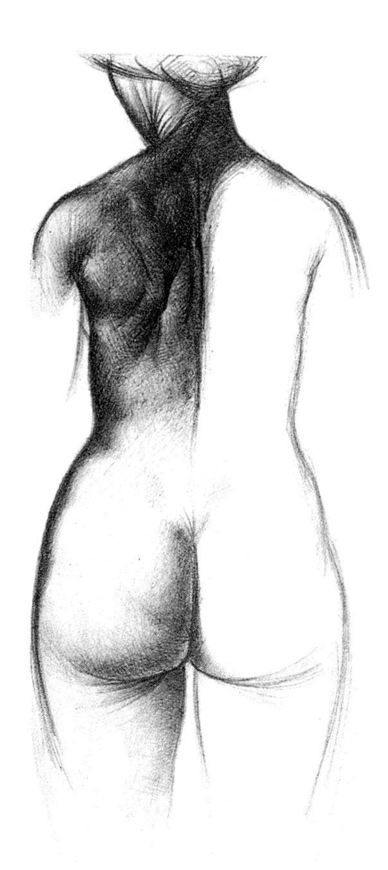

Right: apart from sexual differences, muscular structure depends very much on how the individual has developed it. This drawing of a professional boxer shows how the muscles of his upper arm have been developed to an enormous size by constant exercise.

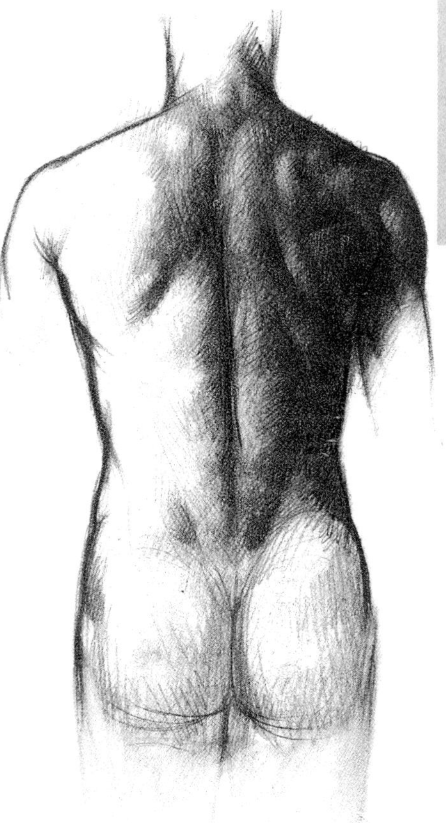

Above, right and far right: the muscular system affects the shape of the human body differently from person to person, and between men and women. The waist is the narrowest part of the body in both sexes, but the shoulders are much narrower in the female form and the hips are usually much broader. The muscles in the upper body are usually more pronounced in the male, and there are generally more areas of fat on the female body, which disguise the muscles.

Not all women and men would fit into the shapes shown here. The idea of the female form being generally pear-shaped, for example, is not always true. What you must do is recognize the general rules, and then observe your model's particular physical make-up very carefully when you draw it.

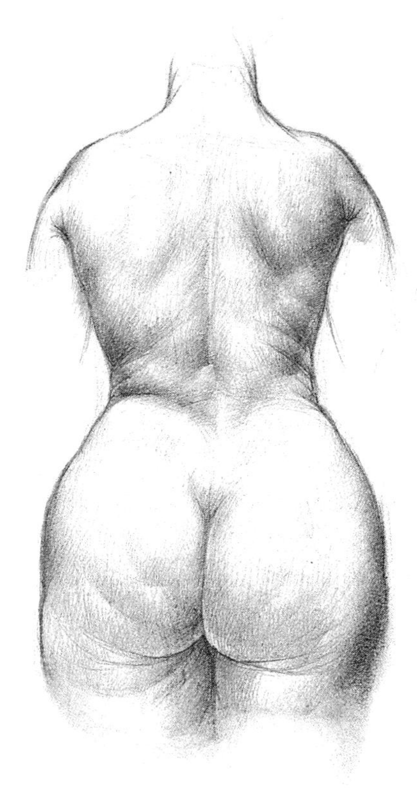

ARTICULATION AND AXES

Because the human body has two sides to it, when even one very small movement is made on one side, the other side has to compensate in some way. It is all about balance. Being aware of this will help you to understand the articulation of the body and its axes of movement.

Left, right and below: these little stick men show how the skeleton articulates when performing actions of various kinds, holding a jar, pulling a rope or hauling a sack. We can see from them how the body balances itself to compensate for the weight or force of its action.

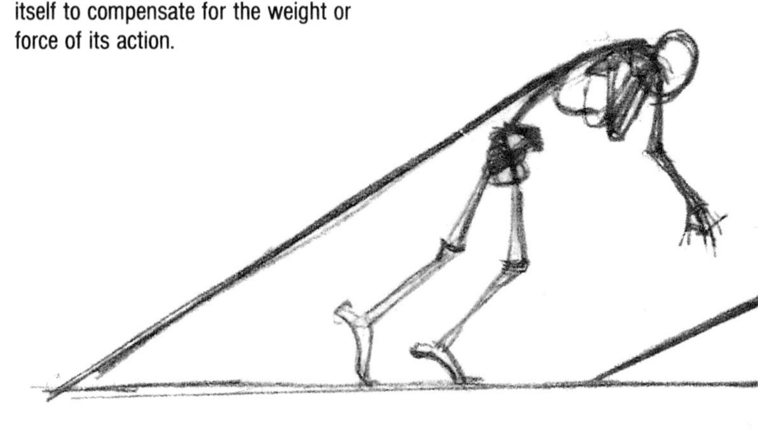

The articulation of the body occurs at all the obvious pivotal points or joints, such as the neck, shoulders, elbows and wrists, knees and ankles. An understanding of the limitations of movements made from each of these points is essential and you will achieve this by careful observation.

The axes are the major horizontal lines of the body, the two most important being the line of the shoulders and that of the hips. These two axes are central to the body's shape as it moves and will give you a firm basis from which to measure other axes.

The first things that you should establish when you start to make a drawing are the axes, no matter how quick and simple your drawing is going to be. It can be helpful to mark them out very lightly on your paper as "directional lines".

Eccentric as it may seem, I often try to imitate the position of the model myself before I draw it, just to get a sense of exactly how all the elements fit together.

Right: this is the theory of the stick man put into practice. You can see from the diagram on the far right how the two sides of the body correlate when the weight is shifted from one foot to another. When you start drawing, try making faint lines like this to appreciate how the two sides correspond. Draw lines along the axes of the shoulder blades, buttocks, knees and heels. Perhaps experimenting first with a stick man diagram in the corner would help.

PROPORTIONS

The rules for the proportions of the human body are guidelines only, but they are a good premise to keep in the back of your mind when you begin drawing.

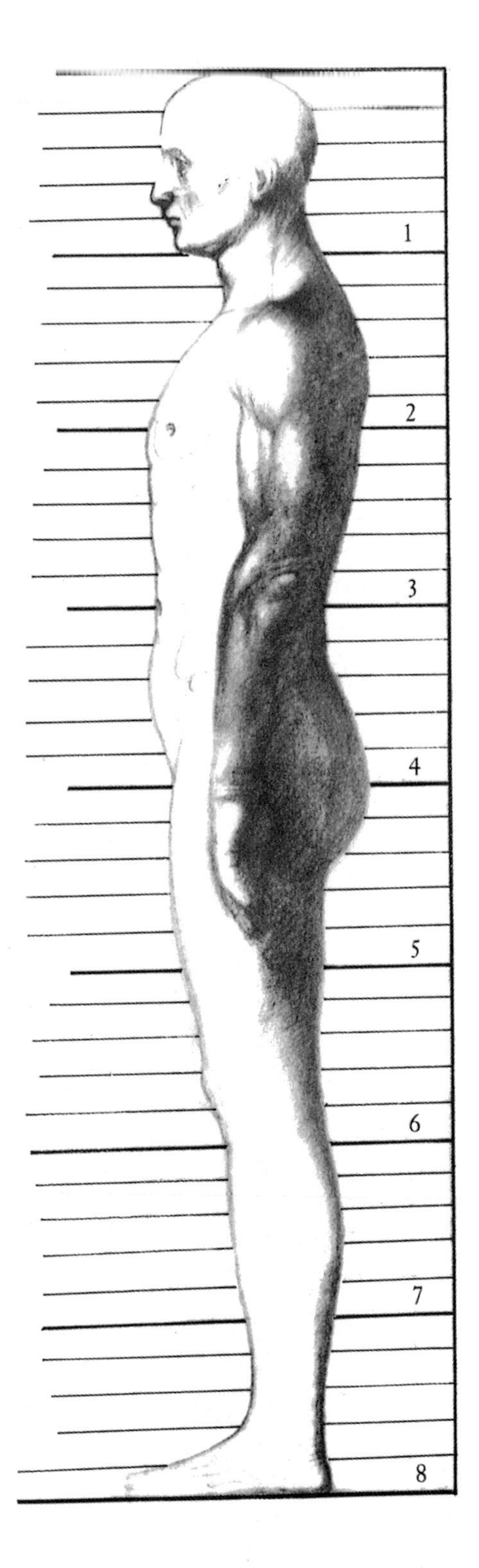

Left: the Renaissance painters believed that the average human body was eight times the head length. This drawing illustrates how odd the figure looks if this rule is adhered to slavishly. However, some rules are useful when you first begin to draw. For example, approximately four heads should fit into the distance between the top of the head and the wrists, and about five and three-quarter heads fit between the top of the head and the knees.

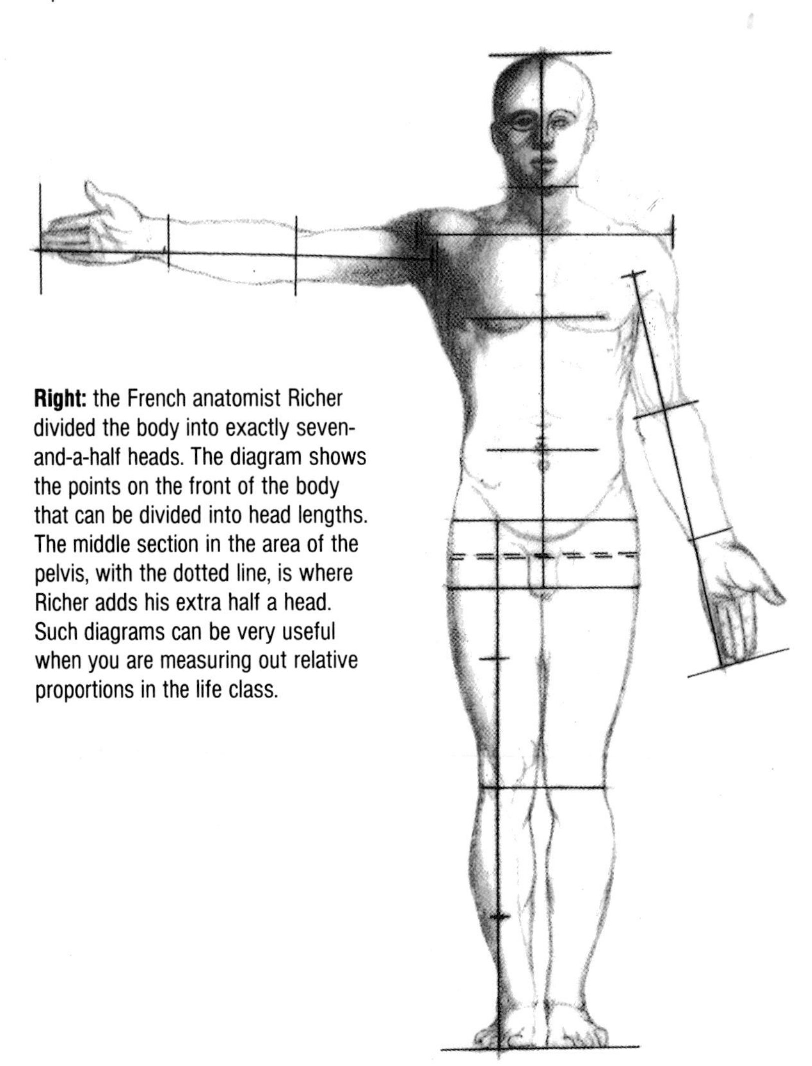

Right: the French anatomist Richer divided the body into exactly seven-and-a-half heads. The diagram shows the points on the front of the body that can be divided into head lengths. The middle section in the area of the pelvis, with the dotted line, is where Richer adds his extra half a head. Such diagrams can be very useful when you are measuring out relative proportions in the life class.

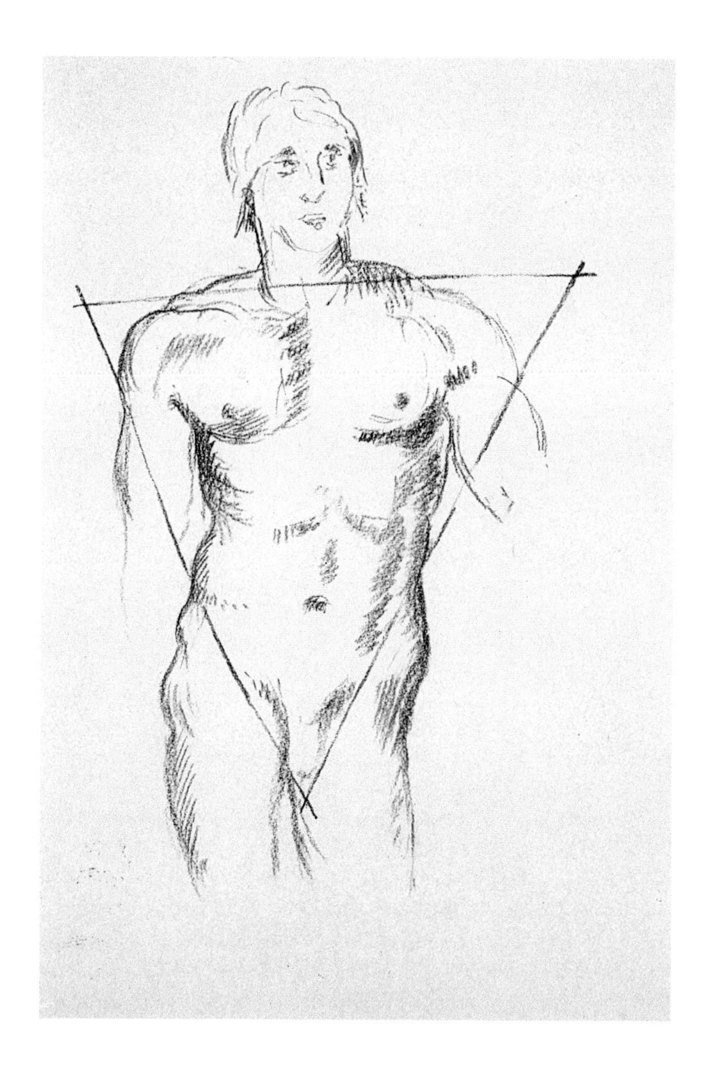

The proportions of the human form were studied by the Classical Greeks, and later taken up by the great Renaissance artists, who developed formulas for them. Basically, the Renaissance theory was that the average body measures seven-and-a-half to eight head lengths, and that the outstretched arms roughly equal the length of the body.

I tend to feel that all this elaborate measuring is cheating and gives a very mechanical result, and that with plenty of practice a sense of proportion will become second nature. Even so, when you are beginning to draw, exact measuring can help to establish a natural feel for proportions.

One useful exercise is to draw the body on graph paper. Start with an important area, such as the head or shoulders and put that down in a square on the grid. Then, using your thumb on your pencil to mark the size of the square, measure off all the other points of the body.

I often use my pencil held up to the model to judge the horizontal or vertical lines of the model's shape and to make sure that I get my lines going at the correct angle.

Whether you are working to a formula or not, do be aware of the relationships between every one of the parts that you draw. The body exists and works as a whole, and is not made up of independent segments.

Above: these diagrams show the difference between the average male and the average female figure. The male form is basically an inverted triangle, whereas the female shape is essentially a triangle or pyramid. The shoulders are emphasized in the male, and the hips in the female.

THE HEAD AND NECK

When drawing the human figure, many beginners concentrate only on the body itself. But the head and neck, too, are a vital part of a model's pose. Their angle can be very expressive of a person's character or mood.

Below and right: the skull viewed from the side and the front has a very distinctive shape which we tend to ignore when it is covered with muscle, skin and hair. Note the large holes where the eyeballs fit, and the fact that the jawbone takes up a much larger area of the basic head shape than we are normally aware of. The projection of the back of the skull is clearer too.

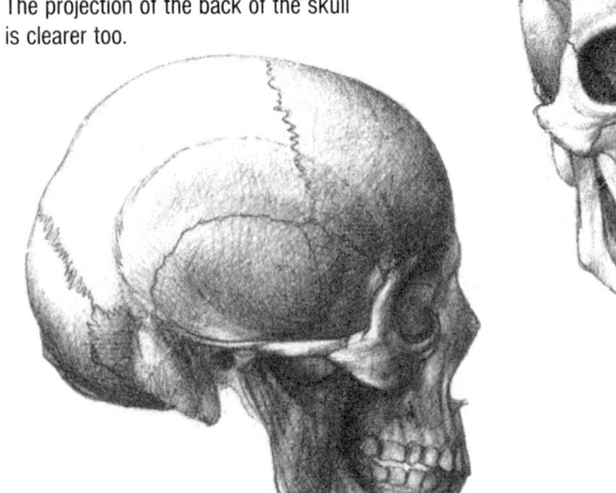

When drawing the head and neck, try to think of the head as basically an oval shape supported by the cylinder of the neck. Once you have established their shape and set, then you can tackle the features.

And tackle them you should. When I see the traditional art school faceless oval staring out at me, devoid of features, I often ask "What is the point of a figure drawing without a face?" The answer really amounts to this – that it is simple to draw and doesn't have to be an exact likeness of the model.

But faces give so many subtle clues to things such as mood, atmosphere and the position of the head and body. A face also helps us, as viewers, to identify with the image. For the artist it is a means of communicating his or her ideas.

I must also stress the importance of hair. It is an essential part of the head and must be drawn together with it, and not merely added as an afterthought. Hair gives us an impression of the age and personality of the model. It can also often seem to increase or decrease the size of the head itself, by its sheer bulk, or lack of it, which affects the character of the person portrayed.

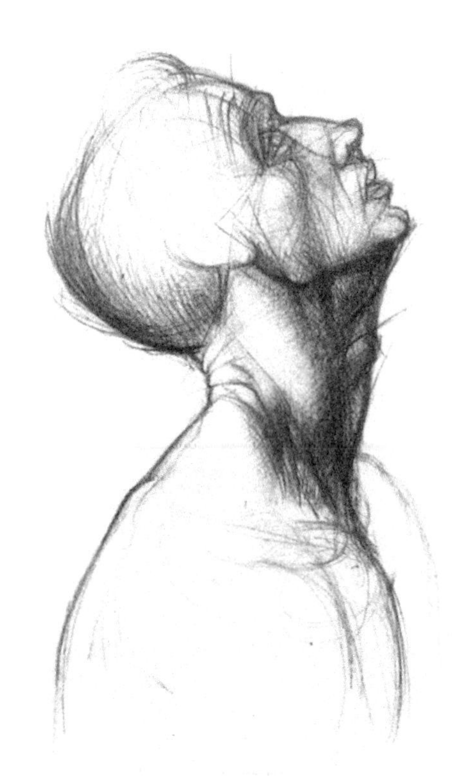

Right: these two drawings emphasize the importance of the neck in supporting the heavy weight of the head. Often, the beginner forgets this important point. Study these drawings carefully to appreciate how the neck changes shape as the head is raised and lowered.

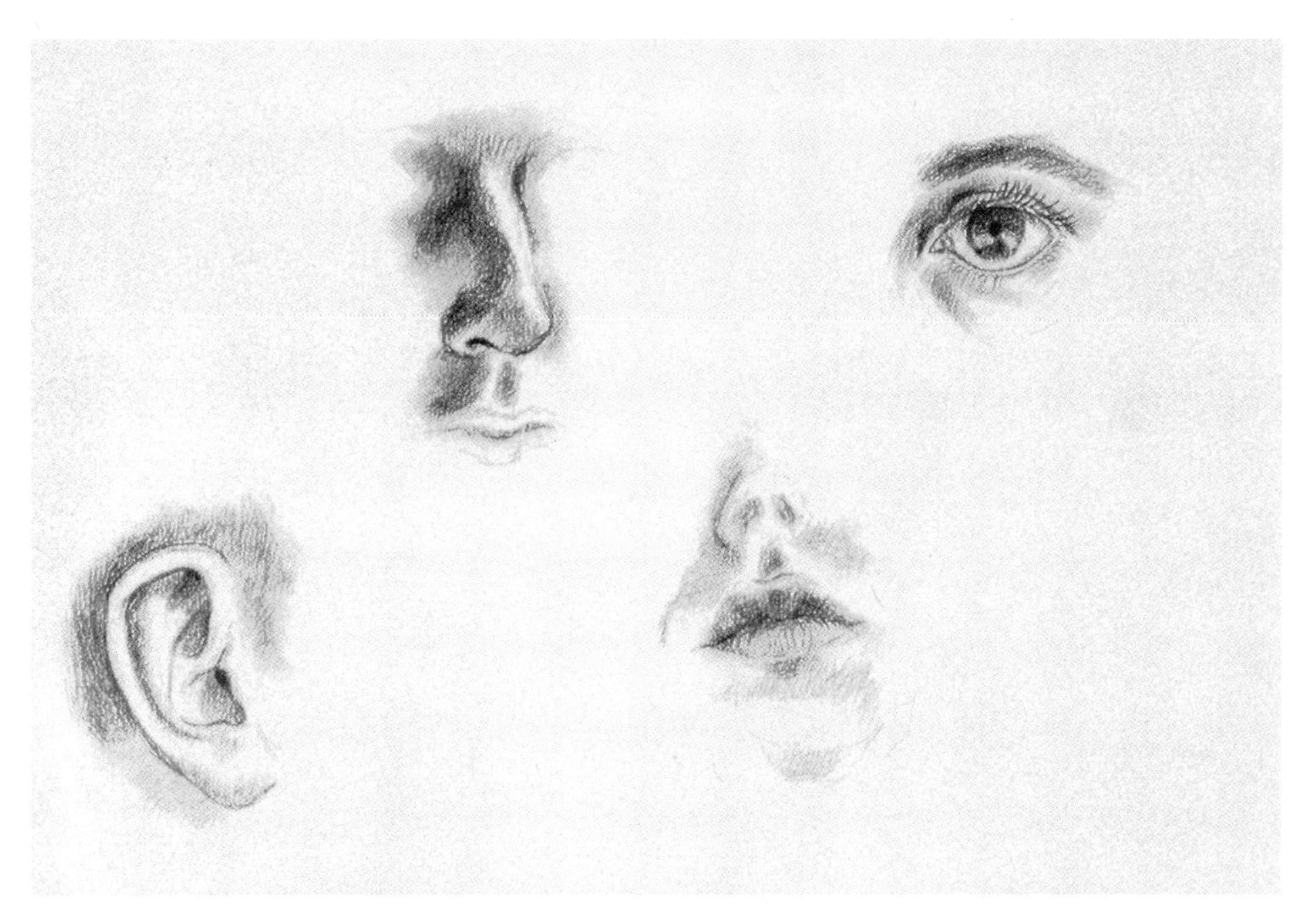

Left: this is a very strong neck, belonging to a professional boxer. His muscles have been developed through plenty of exercise and training to build up strength in the shoulders. This drawing shows how closely connected the muscles of the neck are with those of the shoulders. In this figure, the neck almost takes on more importance than the head.

Above: it is a good exercise to study the features of the face individually, to appreciate the variety of their shapes. Several of these were self-portraits, drawn by looking into a mirror. The lips were drawn at a slightly foreshortened angle, but the other features were drawn face on. Try to draw facial features from many angles. Bear in mind, when drawing the eyes, that the eyeballs are spherical, which affects the shape of the eyelids stretched over them. Also, don't add ears to a face as an afterthought, because this can result in making the overall area of the head enormous. Measure the ears carefully as a proportion of the head area.

HANDS AND FEET

Hands and feet are parts of the body that are commonly left off drawings of figures. This is a mistake because, apart from the face, they are the most expressive parts of the body. They are also its natural "endings".

The reason for leaving out hands and feet is, often, because they are quite complicated to draw. Even the portrait painters of the eighteenth and nineteenth centuries would charge more for an image with two hands rather than one because of this. However, if you reduce hands to a basic shape, they can be quite easy to draw. Get plenty of practice by drawing your own hands, clutching a pencil perhaps, holding a glass or clenched into a fist.

The feet too are very important, particularly in a standing pose, because they take all the weight of the figure. Feet form a natural base to most figure drawing. As with the hands, just regard feet as a shape without worrying about individual toes.

A common fault is to make hands and feet too small. As an exercise to overcome this, try making them larger than they actually are.

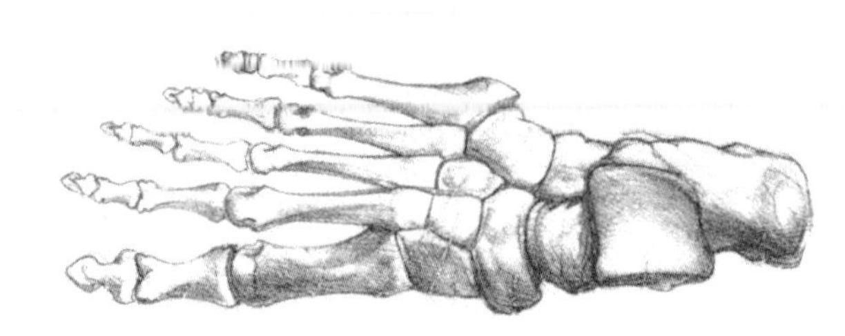

Below left: this diagram of the bones of the hand shows how the joints correspond to one another and demonstrates the large gap between the thumb and forefinger.

Above: the bones of the foot are shown here. It is surprising to see the length of the bones when most of us think of the toes as tiny objects. When drawing the foot, treat it as an overall shape before observing it in more intricate detail.

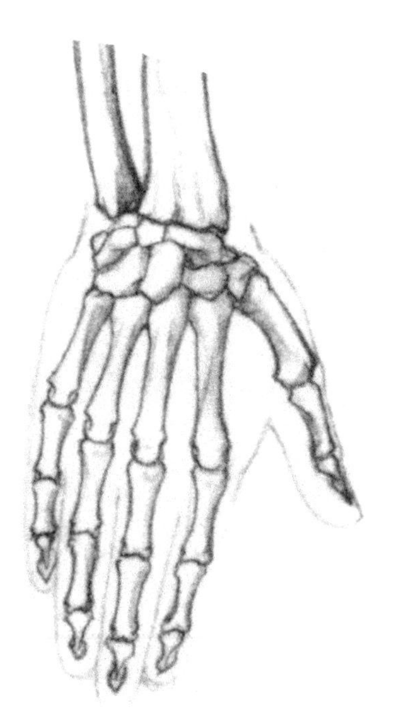

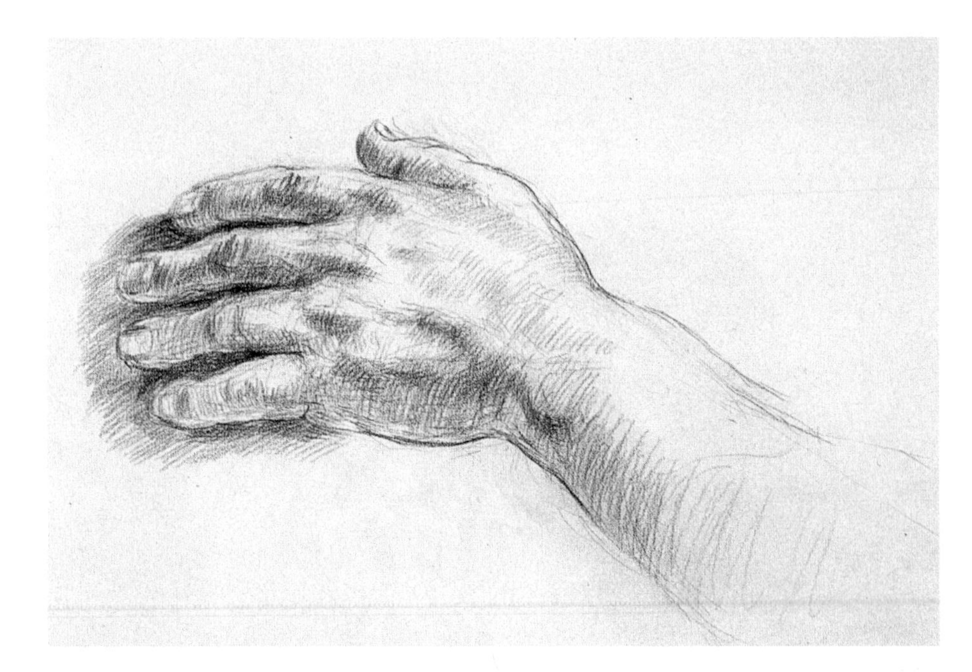

Above: in a drawing of a hand, the knuckle and wrist joints are obvious even when covered with flesh and skin. Draw the hand as a basic shape first before treating the fingers separately.

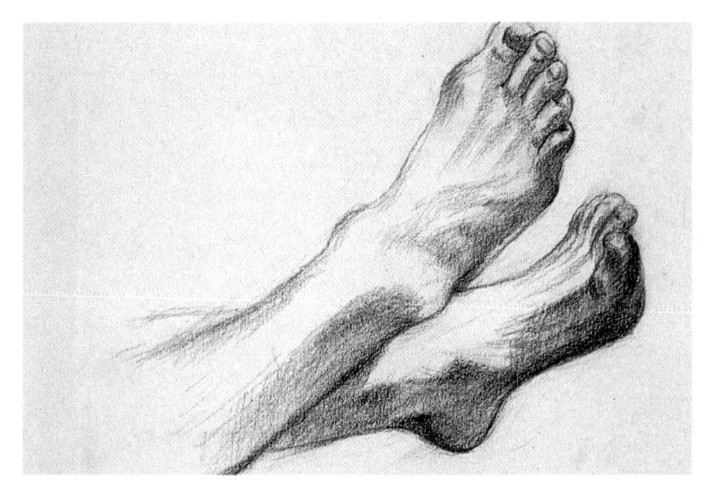

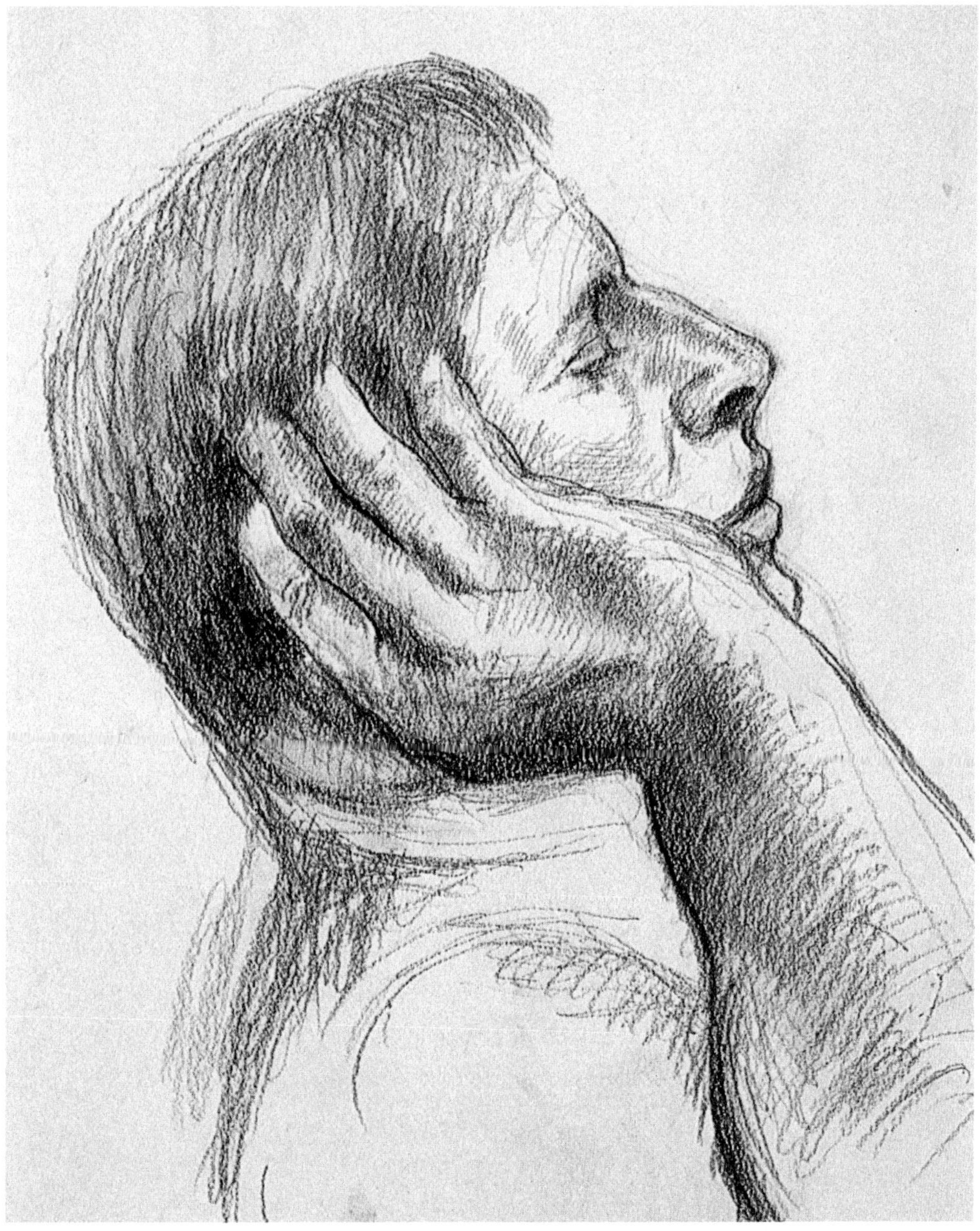

Above left: I asked a friend to take his socks off so that I could draw his feet while he was watching television. Take every opportunity you can to draw, when you have a few moments to spare.

Above: the artist drew his mother's feet while she was doing her ironing, barefoot. It shows what a solid base the feet are and their importance in a standing pose.

Left: this picture demonstrates how expressive the hands are and how large they are in comparison to the head. Try to draw yourself from a mirror with your hands touching your head in different ways. You will make your drawings much more meaningful and convincing if you can put in the hands and feet, difficult though it may be!

FORM AND VOLUME

When drawing the figure, to give it an impression of solidity, of three-dimensionality, you give it form and volume. Although the main method of conveying this quality lies in applying light and tone to your drawing, it should also be visible in the first marks you make.

Right and below: these simple pencil drawings describe basically the roundness and solidity of the human form. In the drawing on the right, the artist has drawn imaginary circles around the rib cage and arms to show this. In the picture below, solidity is conveyed, not with these imaginary lines, but by the sheer weight of the model on her buttocks instead.

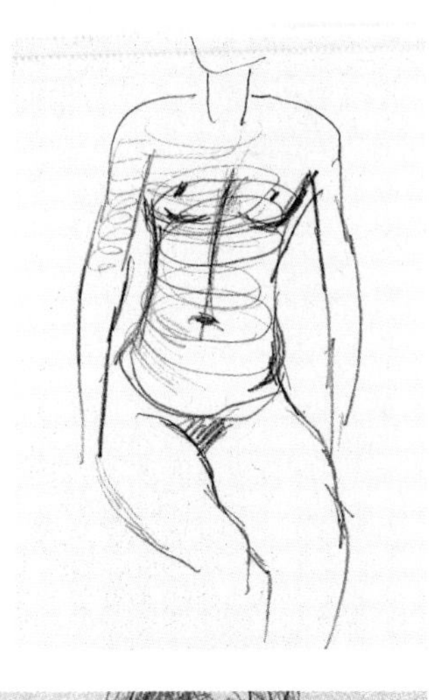

Beginners often think that the trick of giving a figure volume is to "shade it in". They are mistaken, because it will be obvious that the shadows and moulding were an afterthought and the figure will not be convincing.

The way to give volume to your figures is to "feel" the shapes as you draw them. Concentrate on their roundedness. This will give the impression that the shape continues behind the image you have drawn, that it has another side to it.

Left and right: it is very hard to describe form and volume except in a visual sense, and an appreciation of what they really mean can only come with practice. In these two drawings you can feel a sculptural, three-dimensional solidity. In the image on the left, you are convinced that the full weight of the model is on the ground – this has a lot to do with her volume and the shape of her pose. In the figure on the right you can feel the weight of the model in the chair. The artist conveys this by actually drawing around the shapes and stressing the basic cylindrical, conical and spherical shapes that the body is made up of.

LIGHT AND TONE

There are times when a purely linear approach to your work is not sufficient, and you will have to consider light and tone. Together with shadows they give your drawings a sense of solidity and a mood.

You quite often see artists narrowing their eyes, or squinting, while they are drawing. This is so that they can determine the main direction of light on their subject and sort out the tonal values in the scene they are trying to represent. Squinting has the effect of heightening the contrasts between light and dark.

Light is easy to understand. It comes from a given direction, hits a surface and lightens or even highlights it. If you observe carefully and draw what you see, you should be able to tell from your finished drawing exactly where the light source was.

Tone, on the other hand, is a little more difficult to appreciate. It is the area of a solid form that is not directly illuminated.

Shadows are also an important concept to grasp. They are simply the shapes of solid objects projected onto another surface by a light source.

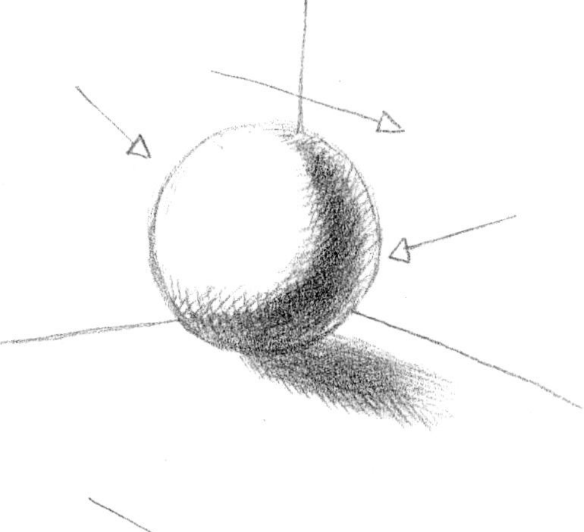

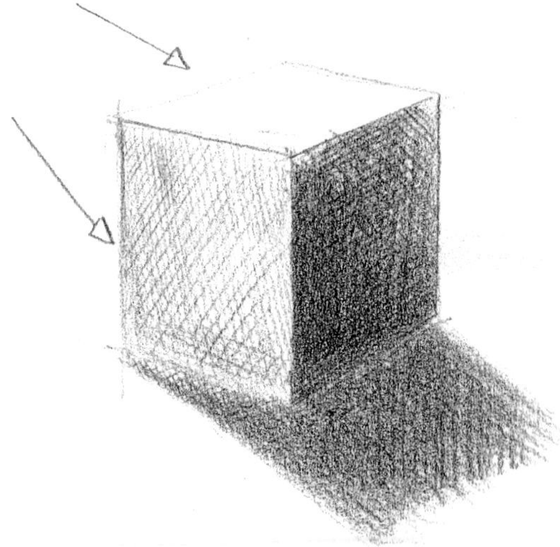

Above: tone and shadow are created when a light hits a surface. High-key tones are produced where light strikes a surface, and middle and dark tones exist where it half-illuminates or does not affect the surface at all.

Left: a pastel drawing of a figure demonstrates the principle of light and tone.

Above: this was one of a series of brush drawings done in a darkened room, using spotlights to create dramatic shadows. The drawings were all done in brush and ink.

Below and right: a thick brush encourages you to concentrate on lighting effects. Use several different strengths of diluted ink in order to describe different areas of tone.

Below: this drawing shows what emotion and feeling can be expressed when light and tone are sensitively employed in a drawing. This was made in conté crayon with areas lightened by an eraser.

VIEWPOINTS AND POSES

You will often see people setting up their equipment in a particular position in the life class without having a clue as to how the model will be posed. My advice to you is – don't do this. Don't just sit down and start drawing without considering the possible viewpoints.

Have a long, hard think about the best viewpoint. Walk around the model for a while, sit on the floor, or stand on a table. Ask yourself if the model looks more dramatic from behind, or from the side.

When you get the opportunity to pose the model yourself, think about the fact that even a simple alteration of position, such as the shift of weight from one leg to another, can alter the character of a pose quite dramatically. Reclining or semi-reclining poses with bent knees and arms throw up all sorts of interesting angles, whereas standing poses are generally simpler but more restricted. A simple article of clothing or a patterned cloth, or the addition of an interesting chair or sofa can transform the scene.

You could also consider having more than one model posing at the same time. The relationship between figures presents marvellous compositional possibilities.

Above and above right: simple seated poses are made slightly different by raising a leg onto the stool, or by crossing the legs.

Right: a very dramatic pose was created when the model was asked to lie on the floor with her hands on her head, while the artist stood above her making drawings.

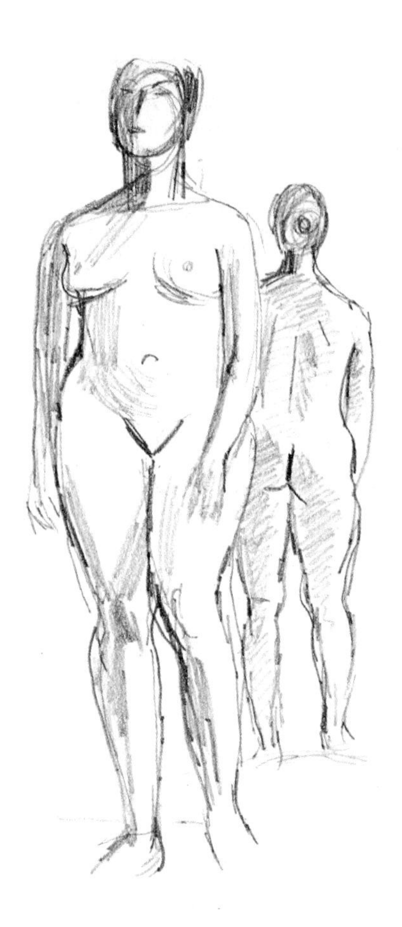

Above: bring other elements into your composition to give it a sense of place and occasion, as has been done here with the studio ephemera. The artist was very fortunate here to have two models to draw and has contrasted their positions – the one being stretched out and the other hunched up.

Above left: a method of making drawings unusual is the use of a mirror, which obviates the need for two models.

Right: the artist focussed closely onto the head, which was drawn at different angles, one of them a difficult foreshortened angle. Try to vary your viewpoint as much as you can. It makes your drawing that bit more personal and your composition more dynamic.

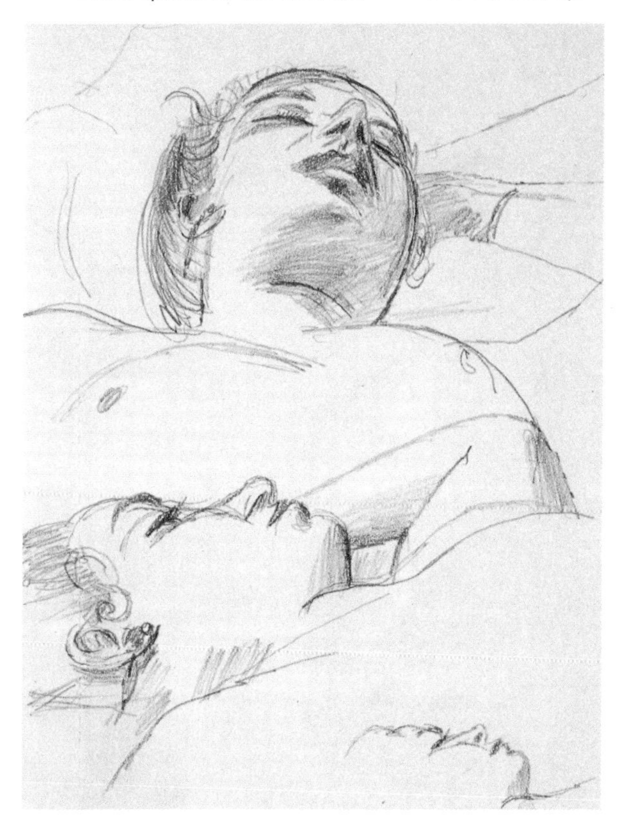

COMPOSITION

In the effort to produce a good drawing, composition is easily forgotten. However, it must come first because, in the end, the impact of your drawing depends on composition alone.

There are all sorts of complicated geometrical theories about composition – the Golden Section is one – but I am not going to go into them. Apart from a few simple rules, your understanding of composition will follow from practice and experience.

The basic thing to remember about good composition is that it must lead the eye into and around the picture, and not out of it.

Above: these four drawings show how, by altering a pose and your viewpoint slightly, you can affect the composition. Here, the gaze of the model draws the eye to the head on the left and back along the model to her head. The composition is essentially a diagonal line between the two heads.

Above: in a similar pose to the one on the left, the head has been removed but the composition is still a diagonal. The dark tone of the knees focusses the eye so that the viewer concentrates on them first.

Above: the strength of the vertical line of the near thigh right in the middle of the picture contrasts directly with the horizontal of the torso. This composition effectively divides the image into two blocks and gives it a solid, geometrical feel.

Above: the whole figure has been fitted into the space available. This can often create a static feel in a composition, but, again, the eye is drawn along the diagonal, from the heavy weight of the dark head to the rectangle of the torso, up to the square of the legs and feet.

Above and right: these two finished drawings are both quite detailed in their own way and both took a long time to create, so the composition had to be right from the start. The top drawing, in pen, ink and wash, concentrates on the shapes created by the two models as well as their surroundings, which it uses to lead the eye around the picture and then back to the focus of attention, the models. The drawing on the right is a simpler composition, concentrating on a single model against a bare background. The artist has used the shadow cast by the figure very effectively to relieve the central position of the figure on the page. The softness of the shadow also counteracts the geometric rigidity of the composition.

MATERIALS

In this section I have described what it is possible to achieve with the many kinds of media available today. I have included details on types of paper because the support is as much a part of the final drawing as the medium. And because "taking away" is just as important as "putting down", I have also discussed the effects of various erasers and knives.

Experimenting and practising with these techniques is really the only way to learn and find out what suits you best in different situations and under different conditions. Try out different combinations of media – there are no hard and fast rules, and every artist has his or her own way of using a favourite medium. Do remember, though, that above all you should remain true to the materials. Don't try to make one medium do what another would achieve a lot better.

PAPER

Professional artists are very particular about paper and often become attached to one kind. You will also probably do so in time. Remember that all papers are manufactured for a particular purpose and the type of paper that you use will affect the way you draw quite dramatically.

There are literally hundreds of different types of paper available. Handmade papers are the most expensive, but machine-made papers are perfectly adequate for drawing. Because they are less expensive, they will not intimidate you as much as a very costly paper can. Your local artists' supplier or paper dealer should be able to tell you exactly what is available.

When choosing your paper, think about what you will be using it for. I have often seen a novice painter struggling to use charcoal on shiny newsprint bought in the interests of economy alone – because the charcol merely glides across the surface.

Shiny paper with a smooth surface is not good for a dry medium such as chalk or charcoal because it doesn't provide sufficient "tooth" for the pigment to stick to. On the other hand, a very rough surfaced paper is not suitable for pen and ink because there is too much tooth, and the surface produces a wobbly and therefore uncontrollable line.

"Badger" handmade paper has an uneven texture which, when worked on in pencil, produces interesting effects.

"Hot" or Cold Pressed paper has a rough surface which creates greater contrasts of texture.

The smooth surface of Hot Pressed paper provides a soft texture for pencil.

Ordinary cartridge/drawing paper has a fairly smooth surface.

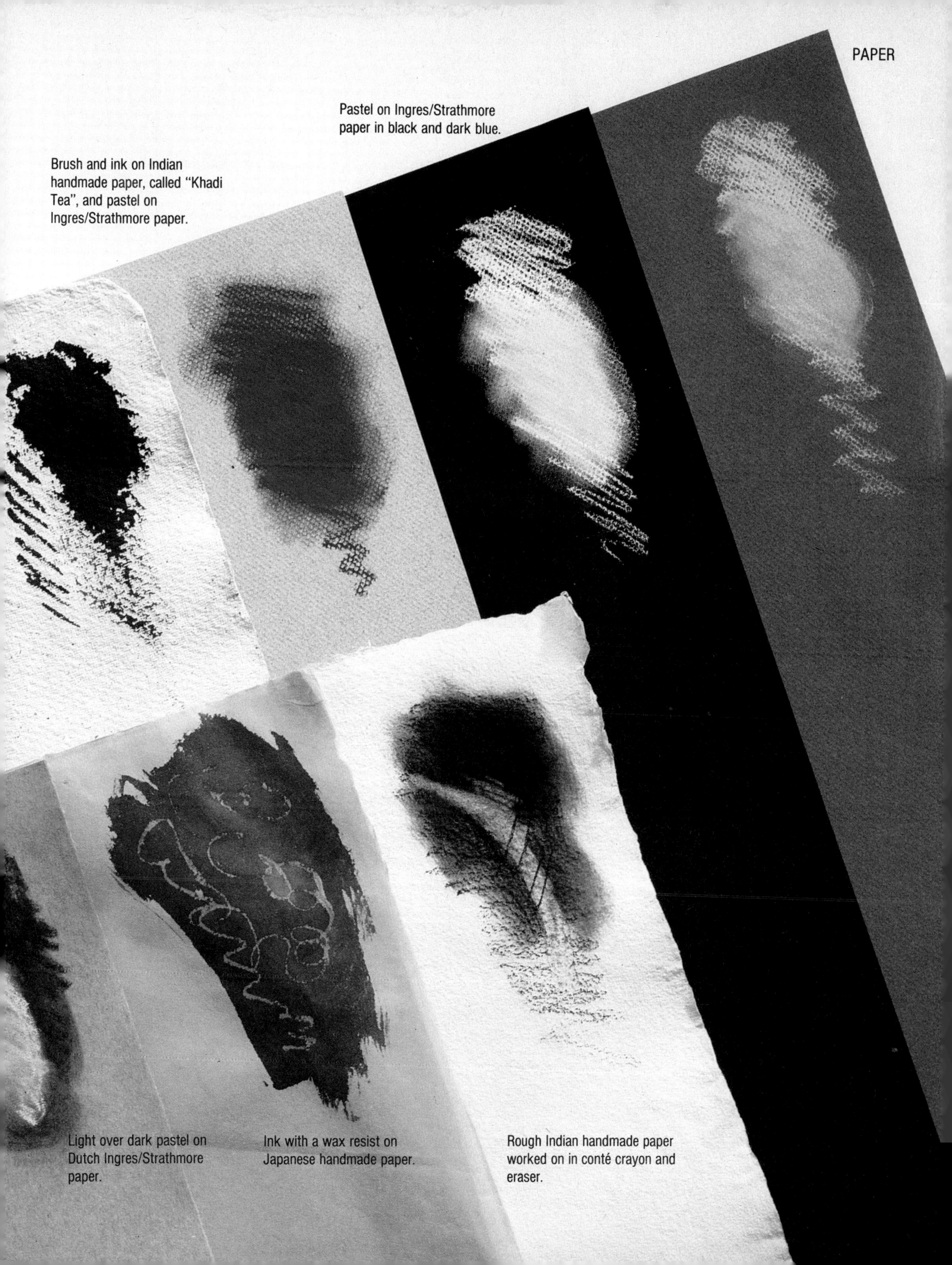

Pastel on Ingres/Strathmore paper in black and dark blue.

Brush and ink on Indian handmade paper, called "Khadi Tea", and pastel on Ingres/Strathmore paper.

Light over dark pastel on Dutch Ingres/Strathmore paper.

Ink with a wax resist on Japanese handmade paper.

Rough Indian handmade paper worked on in conté crayon and eraser.

PENCIL, GRAPHITE AND ERASERS

Pencil and graphite are very direct and simple media. Easily transportable and fairly clean, they allow you to produce a large range of lines and marks, some of which are demonstrated here. They can also be smudged, erased and scraped away, and are therefore ideal for figure drawings.

Ordinary wooden pencils contain solid graphite, which is also available in sticks and comes in degrees of hardness. Graphite sticks are very useful because, being quite thick, they allow you to cover a large area in one stroke. They can also be sharpened to a point, giving you the potential of a very thick or thin line.

Try not to use a sharpener on your pencils, because it tends to break the lead. It is far better to use a craft knife.

Interesting effects can be achieved using an eraser in conjunction with a pencil or a stick of graphite. If you cover your paper or an area of the paper with graphite you can then "draw" into it with an eraser.

Erasers also come in varying degrees of hardness. The softest kinds are putty rubbers/kneadable erasers, which are very malleable; they can be broken off into smaller pieces and rolled to a point. The hardest kinds are ink erasers – they can take away the surface of the paper if you are not careful.

The rougher the paper, the easier it will be to use an eraser on it – very smooth papers just tend to produce a smudge.

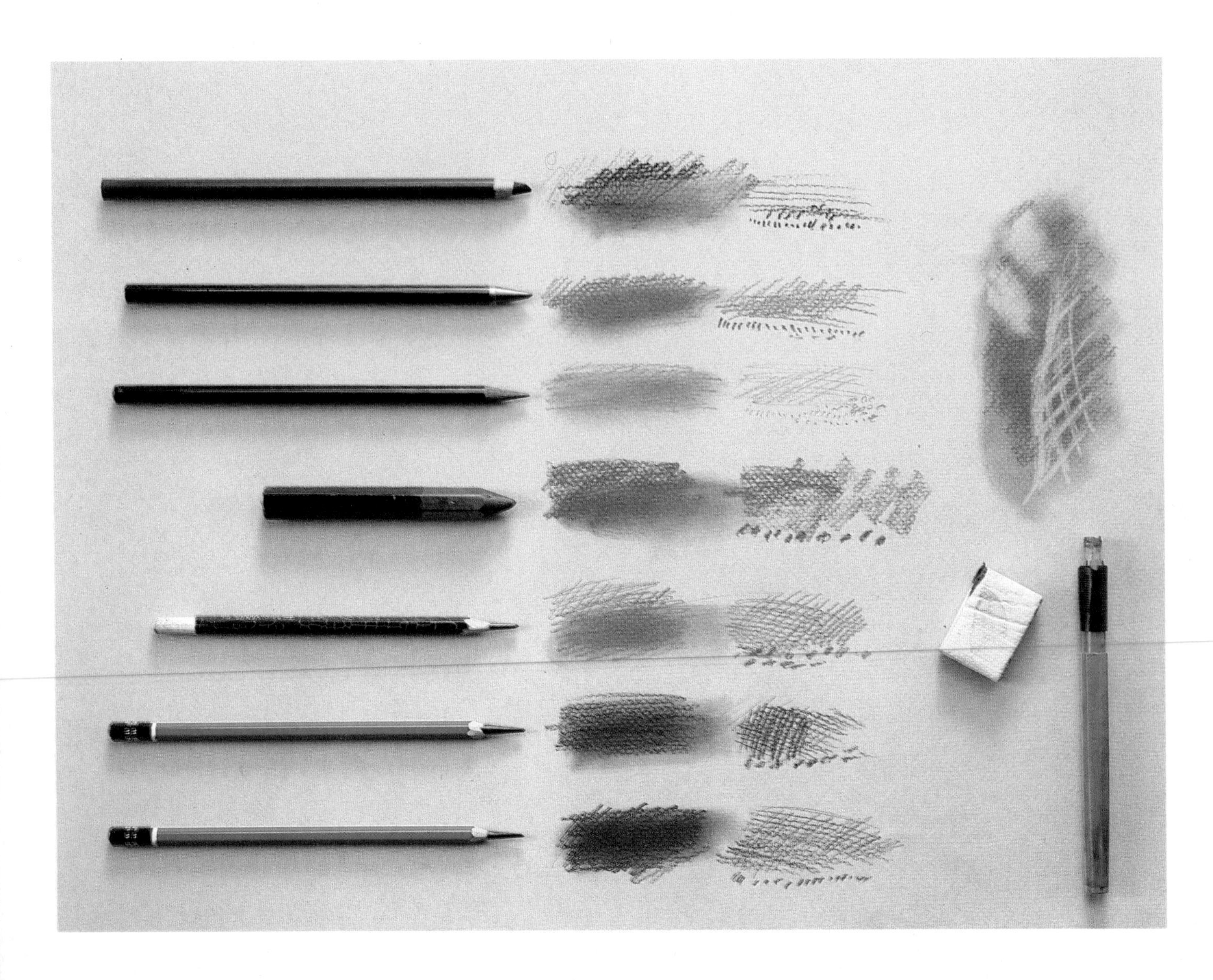

Below: this self-portrait by Peter Evans was drawn in ordinary pencil. The tonal effects have been achieved by building up the density of lines in certain areas and leaving others blank. On the right of the picture you can see how he has studied the head to establish its basic features, while making the main picture.

Above: this drawing was made with EE and EB pencils on smooth sketchbook paper, and shows the darkness of line these pencils produce.

Left: the different kinds of pencils and graphite available create a variety of marks on rough-textured paper. From the top, the pencils are charcoal pencil; a 9B graphite pencil, which has a luxuriously dark and flowing line; a harder, HB, graphite pencil; a graphite stick, which can be used to make broad lines; an ordinary 6B pencil; and two unusual pencils, the EE and the EB – which give a very dark line. Also illustrated are a putty rubber/kneadable eraser and a stick eraser. Above them are the different marks each makes on an area of pencil.

Top: a metalworker at a locomotive depot, drawn with graphite. The artist worked into the graphite with an eraser to achieve the sense of illumination around the head.

Left: a very clean, clear pencil drawing of a seated nude shows how simple, but expressive, pencil can be.

Above: pencil has been used here to produce simple lines, and tone is indicated by massing the lines together. The artist has used a variety of marks in this picture to convey texture and pattern, particularly in the model's hair and in the suggestion of pattern on the cloth that she is lying on.

Left: in this drawing, by Clare Jarrett, pencil lines have been built up very darkly to give a particularly solid, three-dimensional effect. The light source was obviously coming from the right, towards the model's face, giving the model a statuesque beauty. Certain areas have been left entirely blank, but in leaving out detail they still manage to describe the forms.

Right: this drawing was made with a graphite stick, used on its side in parts, almost as a kind of wash, and on its point to produce lines. The end result is very painterly and reflects the subtlety of the medium. The greys that it gives are very delicate and shiny.

CHARCOAL

Charcoal is the most painterly of all the drawing media. It is quite difficult to control because of this but it is very versatile. It can be used in broad passionate strokes and even to make quite detailed drawings.

Charcoal is made of charred willow. It comes in pencil form and in sticks, from very thin sticks to the fat chunks of what is called "scene painters' charcoal". Sticks of charcoal are also manufactured from compressed powder.

Charcoal can be sharpened to a point, either with sandpaper or a craft knife, and used to create meticulous detail. Alternatively, you can use its edges and thickness to create broad, expressive marks.

You can take elements away from your charcoal drawing quite easily, or smudge and blend its marks to add to it, with a piece of rag or an eraser. This is all part of the fun of using charcoal.

Left: this picture of a girl in a chair was made using a sharpened piece of charcoal. The point was probably made by rubbing the charcoal on a sheet of fine sandpaper. The result shows that charcoal need not be a clumsy or even a painterly medium, but can be controlled to produce a clean, linear image.

Above: charcoal is used here in a very tender and delicate way, just as line, with no tone applied at all. Charcoal works very well like this because if you make a mistake you can easily remove it with a finger, leaving an almost clean surface underneath. The medium is so light that it does not damage or permanently mark the surface of paper.

Left: quite thick, Arches paper has been used for this drawing by Bernadette Coxon, in which charcoal has been applied in its most familiar way. The dramatic lighting and sculptural effect in this image express great atmosphere. Be prepared, when working on a heavily textured surface like this, for your stick of charcoal to wear down very quickly!

CONTE AND CHALK

Conté and chalk are ancient media and have been used by many of the Great Masters, including Michelangelo, Rubens and Claude. There is a great deal of confusion over the difference between the two, because they come in many similar forms.

Basically, conté is a stick made from pigment mixed with gum and a tiny amount of grease. It is harder than chalk and comes in a wider variety of colours. Chalk, on the other hand, is quarried straight from the ground and is like the schoolroom chalk that we know today. It comes mainly in grey, white, black, red and brown, and is sold in either pencil or stick form.

Conté and chalk can be used in a linear way for a graphic effect, or in a very painterly way, especially when smudged. Popular with early artists precisely because of their painterly nature, they could also be used for preparatory drawings prior to a painting and give an impression of the final effect that would be achieved. These preparatory works, or cartoons, were usually done in red chalk or conté, which was heightened with white to give solidity to the forms.

Far right: a conté crayon drawing on brown paper, heightened with chalk. Some pastel has been used for the blue of the socks.

Left: this outstretched nude male was drawn on very light brown paper. You can see what a strong line the conté crayon gives without being clumsy. Conté can be sharpened to a point to work quite a lot of detail into the image.

Below: a conté crayon called pierre noir was used for this drawing. It comes in pencil form or as a sort of propelling/mechanical pencil.

PEN AND INK

Pen and ink is often considered to be an inflexible and rather mechanical medium. I have found it to be just the opposite. If you use the correct nib in your pen and approach your drawing in a relaxed way, you will find that it can be expressive and sympathetic.

Above: I drew this image with a bamboo pen dipped into sepia ink. As you can see, this medium is capable of a wide variety of beautiful marks. In some areas, such as the hair, I smudged the ink with my finger.

One of the things this medium does is force your total concentration, because any mistake you make has to remain on the page, and this is what frightens people. But it really doesn't matter if you make a mark in error. This all adds to the charm and effect of a pen drawing. Rembrandt was one of the greatest exponents of pen and ink, and you often see areas in his work where lines have been blotted and removed and gone over again and again.

Felt pens, mechanical pens, reed pens, quills and pieces of stick which you sharpen yourself are all considered to be pens. They all give fascinating qualities of line when used with ink.

Pen and ink drawings can be combined very successfully with a wash applied with a brush, either before or after the ink drawing is made. If you are going to try this combination, you must consider first if you are going to use waterproof or non-waterproof ink. Waterproof ink will resist a wash.

Pens come in a variety of forms, from the simple to the sophisticated. Sharpened bamboo, pens with metal nibs, interchangeable fibre-tipped pens, ball pens and fountain pens all make their own characteristic marks.

Above and below: I made these two drawings using a 303 nib and watered-down sepia ink. They show how, with the right nib, a beautifully flowing line can be produced. The image below demonstrates how well this medium combines with a watercolour wash.

Above: this delicate drawing was created with a 303 nib and a wash. With sepia, you can use lots of lines to build up areas of tone or wash it with water to spread it on the paper.

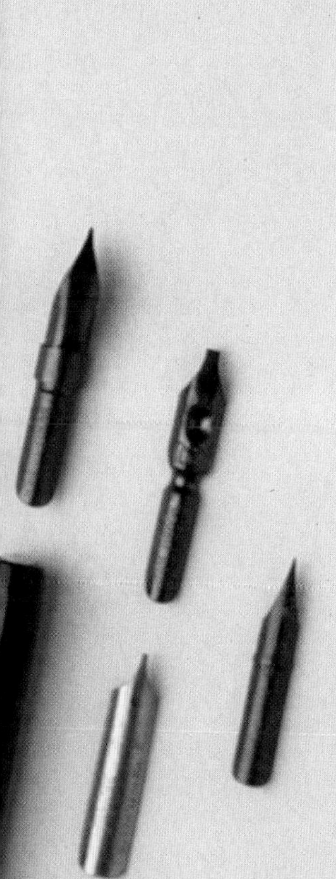

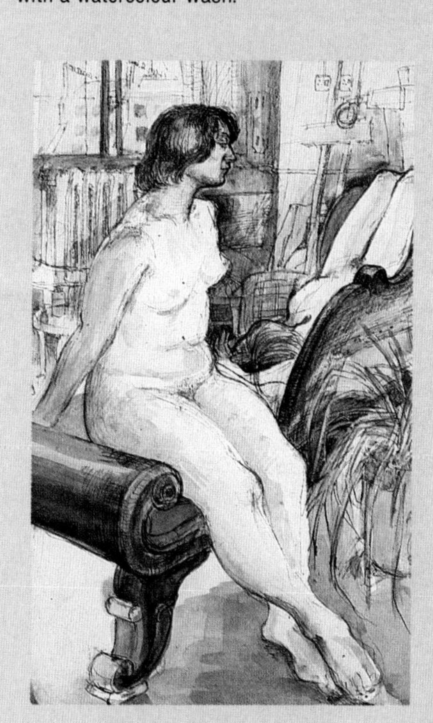

CRAYONS AND WAX CRAYONS

Coloured pencils came into favour only recently, when David Hockney produced a very successful series of portraits using them. In contrast, wax crayons on the whole are not used by professional artists mainly because their colour range is small and the colours themselves tend to be weak. These crayons do have their uses, though.

Using coloured pencils, it is quite difficult to mix colours on the page. To subvert this problem, the manufacturers produce them in a vast range of colours.

Coloured pencils tend to produce a drawing which is essentially linear and quite graphic. However, there are pencils on the market which are watersoluble and therefore provide the opportunity to mix line and wash in the same medium and achieve a more painterly effect. You can spread or apply the watersoluble pigment either with a brush or a rag.

Coloured pencils are not very practical when used on a large scale, because they tend to be a laborious medium. However, they are well suited to small-scale work and sketchbooks. Wax crayons are useful as a resist against watercolour or ink, a technique which has been used often in the works of Henry Moore and John Piper. As a medium on their own wax crayons have been overtaken in popularity by oil pastels.

Right: this image was made with watersoluble pencil crayons, using a small piece of sponge to mix the colours on the page while they were wet. These pencils are very good if you want to work more quickly than ordinary pencil crayon normally allows.

Right: using wax crayon as a resist against watercolour is a very rapid technique which produces some unusual results. However, I suggest that you wait until your drawing hand has "warmed up" a little before you use this technique, because you have to be quite accurate. This medium conveys dramatic lighting effects very well.

Below: the artist has used watersoluble crayons here to produce a combination of vibrant cross-hatching, solid line and wash.

Left: pencil crayon used to build up layers of lines of different colours can produce a variety of shades on the paper. However, this technique is quite laborious and requires a lot of practice.

OIL PASTELS

Oil pastels have a slight clumsy quality which makes them not entirely suited to life drawing because they allow you so little control over the weight of the marks you make. However, when they are used in conjunction with other media, it is possible to achieve spectacular results.

Oil pastels come in a wide range of brilliant colours. You do not need all the colours, though, because you can mix them on the page, either by smudging them, or blending them with turpentine.

I use oil pastel on thick paper with a turpentine wash and as a resist against watercolour or ink. But really they can be used with practically any medium. Their colours are so brilliant that they can hold their own with other media. The pastels themselves also have a very thick and dense texture, which can be scraped into or away with a knife or pen.

Left: oil pastel has been used here as line and also as a wash, mixed with turpentine or white/mineral spirit to move the colour around on the paper. I find that blending the pastel with turpentine makes the medium less rigid and helps me to achieve a greater variety of marks.

Below: oil pastels are manufactured in myriad colours, but you should limit your palette rather than try to make use of all of them.

Above: in this image I have used oil pastel as a resist against a watercolour wash. This method works well with poses that are drawn quickly.

Right: oil pastel has been applied here in the traditional fashion, building up thick layers of colour and then working into them with other colours. Use them when the pose suggests strong colours.

SOFT PASTELS

Soft pastels are a very beautiful medium. They have a pure and brilliant colour because of the way they are made, and allow you to produce large areas of colour quickly. Used with suitable papers, such as Canson or Ingres/Strathmore, which have a slight "tooth" to them, the effect of soft pastels can be quite magical.

Soft pastels are made from pure powdered pigment with a certain amount of resin or gum to bind it together. Certain colours require less gum and so these pastel sticks crumble more easily. This doesn't matter, because you can always push the crumbled pieces into the paper with your finger.

It is possible to use a piece of rag or tissue paper to blend and mix your colours on the paper. The result is a broad "wash" which can then be worked into in detail with a wide variety of media such as conté or charcoal. You can even work into the wash in pastel again, using "torchons". These are twists of paper shaped like tiny thin pencils, made especially for working in pastel.

Your drawing should be fixed layer by layer as you go along so that you can go over certain areas again without destroying the underlying colour. The best fixatives are those you mix yourself and apply with a mouth diffuser.

Despite what some people say, pastel is a very permanent medium if maintained properly. Look at the pastel portraits that were so popular in the eighteenth century. They are still as brilliantly coloured now as the first day they were made.

Left: soft pastels are available in a huge range. They are produced in every colour and in varying degrees of tints and shades of each colour.

Right: this drawing demonstrates most of the marks that a soft pastel can make. The paper worked on is Ingres/Strathmore, which is the most suitable for pastel, in my opinion, because it allows plenty of leeway to mix colours on the paper. The dark red of the paper shows the lighter colours of the pastels to advantage.

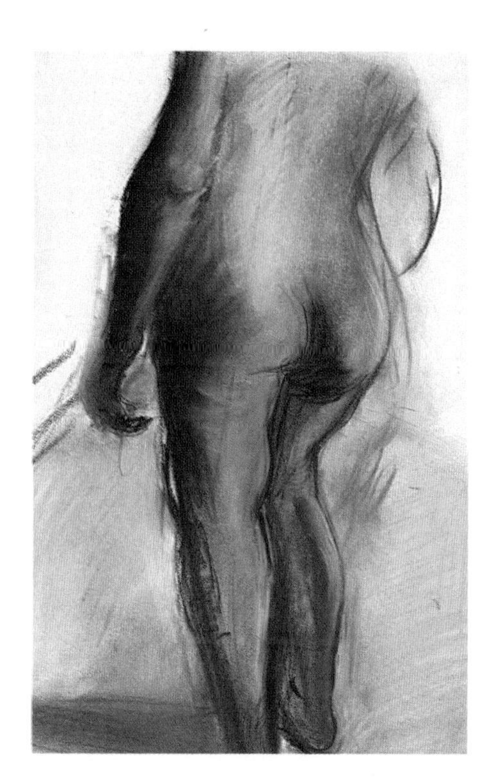

Left and right: these drawings illustrate how strong pastel colours can be. In the image on the left, I applied the pastels in broad sweeps of colour across the page, and then drew on top of them to create a variety of marks. On the right, the drawing of two models shows the luminosity that can be achieved when you work light colours over a dark background.

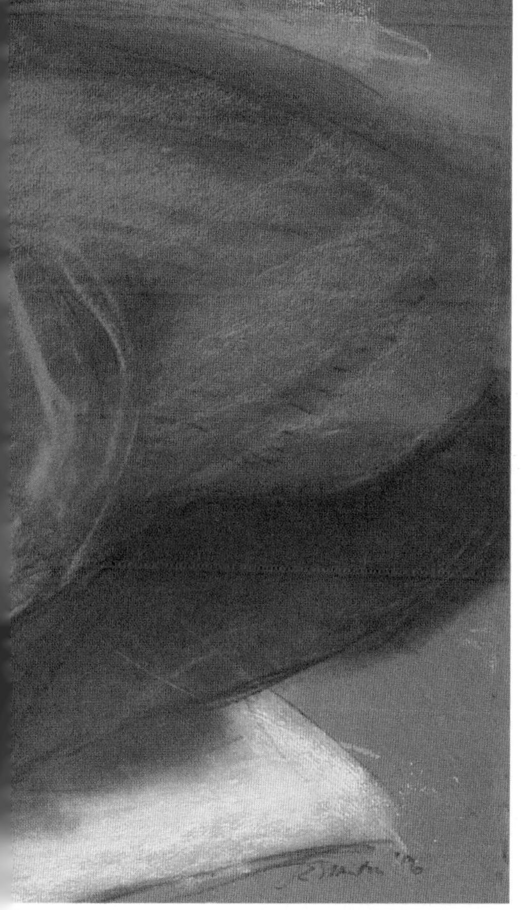

Below: this pastel drawing depicts a man at work in a silkscreen studio. It is a colourful subject which lends itself very well to the powerful colour potential of pastel.

BRUSH DRAWING

A brush is usually associated with painting, but it also makes a very effective drawing tool. You can use oriental or western brushes, with ink or watercolour.

You have to hold your breath a bit when using a brush, because even though the line it produces is very delicate it is also definite and can be difficult to remove once it is on the paper. Drawing with a brush requires lots of forethought and deliberation. However, it is a beautifully expressive medium and I do not want to scare you off. With practice you will discover how rewarding it can be.

I prefer to use a springy, round sable brush, from size 00 to about a number 4. I find that oriental brushes are a bit too limp for my taste. I like a drawing ink such as Chinese ink, which you rub on a slab and mix yourself. You can also buy it ready mixed.

There are many kinds of ink available, both waterproof and non-waterproof. Waterproof inks have shellac in them which gives them a veneer when they dry. Personally, I dislike this, but it can add an interesting texture to your drawing.

It is a good idea to mix several different dilutions of ink, from very dark to light, so that you can make light, tentative marks at the beginning of your drawing and strengthen them with darker ink as you develop the work.

Try working with bristle, or old and damaged brushes; they often give a very beautiful, hesitant line when used semi-wet.

Below: this drawing of a semi-clothed girl lying on a sofa was done with a thin brush and sepia ink. The ink was mixed in several strengths and the artist started with a very light solution. It is not a good idea to draw pencil lines first because you find yourself trying to imitate the marks of the pencil with the brush. It's better to start in ink straight away.

Left: this ink brush drawing was made with ordinary black writing ink, which has a blue tinge to it and is therefore a little less harsh than dense black. The artist has used his brush in different ways to achieve interesting textures.

Below: while the model was resting, the artist quickly drew her with a brush and sepia ink. This medium is very good for swift drawings and produces a beautifully flowing line. I like the subtle effect that the brush has when it is running out of ink and produces a drier line.

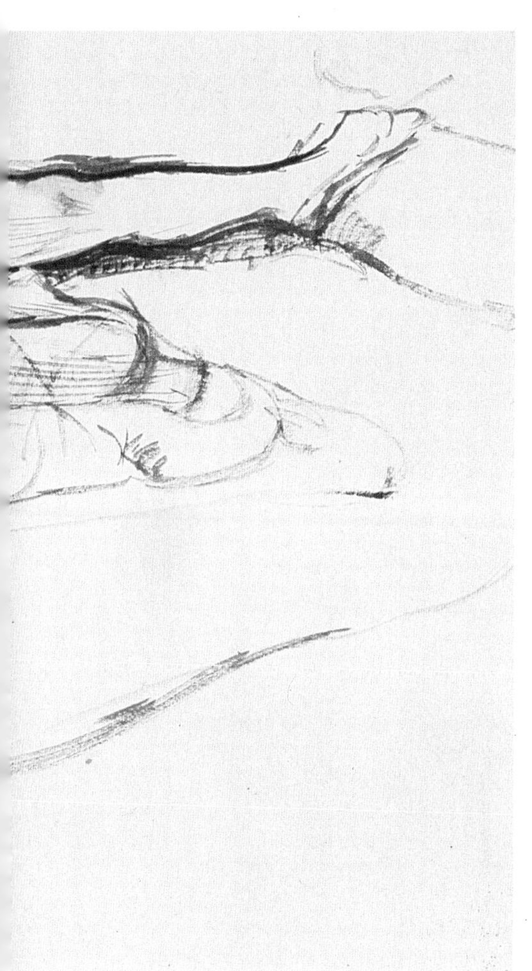

MIXED MEDIA

Many beginners think that if they use one medium on a piece of paper they have to stick to it, but, with a few exceptions, you can mix practically any medium with another, or several others.

There are traditional mixed media, such as pen and wash, or charcoal and white chalk, but you can invent your own. All the best artists had their idiosyncrasies where media were concerned. Van Gogh, for example, drew with special pens fashioned from the hollow twigs of a plant found in the south of France, and Degas often started his pastel drawings with monoprints. Each artist is as individual in his or her choice of materials and method of working as in their choice of subject matter. It is up to you to take a chance and experiment.

The range of unusual materials that you can make a mark with includes tea bags, coffee, burnt toast, sand, glue, waste paper, potato and hand prints, even smoke from a wax candle! You can cut into your picture with a knife, wash it in the bath, sew it with thread, or use household bleach on it, as shown on the opposite page. So, have no fear of departing from the traditionally accepted artists' materials.

Left: this heroically posed male model was drawn in watercolour, ink, white chalk and other media. I particularly like the way that the artist has used the shadow of the arm to add to the drama of the composition. She was obviously so involved in her piece of work that she picked up almost anything that made a mark to do this drawing.

Above: the model was set up in a room lit by red and blue filtered light, which led to the unusual colours of this drawing. This image was made using diluted ink and, in certain parts, pencil.

Right: this is an example of bleach drawing. The technique involves covering your paper with writing ink and then drawing into it with a nylon brush dipped into ordinary, diluted, household bleach. All sorts of effects can be achieved with bleach; it can be drawn on with steel pens or spattered onto the page. Do be careful, though, not to breathe in the fumes or to spill it on yourself.

COLLAGE

Collage is a marvellous medium to use for drawings because the effects it produces can often be unexpected and quite unusual. You can use virtually anything for collage, as long as you can stick it down with glue to your support.

Get into the habit of collecting suitable pieces of discarded materials as you find them – silver foil, old bus and cinema tickets, fruit wrappers, brown paper bags, and magazine cuttings – so that you build up a ready supply of materials that you can use to create all kinds of effects when you come to do your collages.

You will need strong paper, or even better, cardboard, to stick your materials on. Collage is particularly effective when it is used in combination with a traditional drawing medium such as brush or pastel.

Above: Andy Baker began his collage by roughly laying out some basic shapes in paper, based on a life-drawing he made in the studio. You can vaguely make out the impression of a figure at this stage. But the artist kept the composition fairly flexible at the beginning, to make sure that the collage was as spontaneous as possible.

Right: it has become more obvious that a figure will emerge from the shapes. By this stage the artist has made some ink lines in black on the image, to give it more definition as well as to add a further colour into the work.

Left: the final piece is a very exciting and lively portrait of a male figure. Andy has used a variety of materials, including sheets from an old notebook, strips of discarded coloured paper, brown paper packaging and felt pen. There is absolutely no limit to what you can use in collage. It is a good idea to use a drawing you have already made to inspire your piece. But do not try to copy your original slavishly in collage, as it will not necessarily translate well into another medium.

MONOPRINTING

The word "monoprint" means a one-off print and refers to the most direct and simple form of printmaking. Monoprinting is very effective when used as a direct drawing technique, when you are working straight from the model.

There are two methods of monoprinting. For the first you need a smooth surface, ideally a thick piece of glass or a smooth metal plate. Draw onto this surface using a greasy substance, such as printer's ink or oil paint. Then place a piece of paper on top of it and press with a handroller. The result is a reverse impression of your drawing on the glass.

If the surface you use is an etching plate, and the drawing medium is ink, you can put the result through a printing press.

The second method works rather like a carbon copy. Cover a piece of paper with printer's ink and place it inked side down on top of another piece of paper. Then draw on the back of the first piece of paper. This transfers the drawing to your paper underneath, which will be revealed when you peel the two apart. The drawing below was made by the first method.

Left: this brush drawing served as a basis for the following sequence. The artist, Clare, squared it up so that she could copy it.

Right: using the grid on the original drawing as a guideline, Clare drew the image onto a transparent sheet of plastic with black oil paint.

Right: the final image was then printed onto paper. As you can see, it is the reverse of the original image. The artist worked with grey and black paint, and exploited the rich textures that monoprinting can give. All sorts of little accidents happen in the monoprinting process which can be delightful to discover and add a lot of atmosphere to the final picture.

LIVE SITUATIONS

This section discusses the problems that occur when you begin to draw in a less controlled situation than a life class. The model in a class will keep stock still for you, and the studio is usually in total silence. But, when you are working at home, life has to go on around you, and this will test your concentration. So you must not grumble when mum wants to make herself a cup of tea while you are in the middle of producing your masterpiece. Also, if you are not patient, your "models" will run away when they see you getting out your drawing board. I speak from experience! Two other elements are dealt with here – clothes and movement. In real life people do not sit around naked for hours on end. Above all, approach your subjects – family, friends or strangers – in a relaxed, confident manner.

DRAWING FAMILY AND FRIENDS

Members of your family, or friends, as they relax or go about their daily tasks, can make good subject matter for figure drawing. Household activities, such as cleaning the windows, scrubbing the floor, ironing, or cooking are often very interesting to draw. Many of the great artists drew their wives, husbands or lovers eating a meal at the dinner table, or having a bath or wash.

Fortunately for artists these days, the model at home can watch television to alleviate the boredom of modelling, but try to think of more interesting poses then; not sitting or reclining, if your model is willing. Try to draw what your model would be doing normally, such as having a bath, practising a musical instrument, or even having a nap. These very natural, domestic situations can make much more beautiful pictures than a heroic pose in the life class.

You can sort out your own lighting effects by using anglepoise lamps, candles or ordinary bedside lamps to make the setting more dramatic. Use any props you can find in the house, such as curtains, mirrors, cushions or pillows, to add interest and colour.

Left: this is a marvellously gutsy drawing, in charcoal, of the artist's mother concentrating on her ironing. Someone ironing is a good subject to draw because although the figure moves slightly all the time, the movements will be constantly repeated. It is interesting that the iron and the ironing board become almost an essential part of the model herself.

Right and below: these two very heartfelt and delicate portraits are of friends of the artist. The one on the right is in pencil; the drawing below is in conté crayon. Both models are posed in a very natural manner and were probably allowed to watch the television or listen to the radio while the artist worked, as these drawings must have taken quite a long time to do.

Right: try to think of the various angles from which you can study your model. The artist of this drawing has taken a sideways view of the model, which gives a profile of the head that is particularly effective. This drawing was done in conté pencil.

CHILDREN AND BABIES

Children and babies are perhaps the most problematic subject to draw – they soon get bored, and fidget and wriggle around no matter how much you promise them or whatever you bribe them with. The secret is to work quickly and often, and to have all your materials absolutely ready before you begin.

To keep children cooperative, it is a good idea to let them watch television, play a game, read a book, sleep, or even draw you. If you are attempting an ambitious work, it is best to get the child to sit for you on several occasions.

When drawing babies, notice that they have a very large head in comparison to the rest of their body, and a relatively thin and frail neck. They also have very rounded, large cheeks, and their lips tend to protrude more than their other features, in order to make it easier to suckle. The features are crowded into a small area of the face.

This appearance is the same for children, but is less and less exaggerated as they get older.

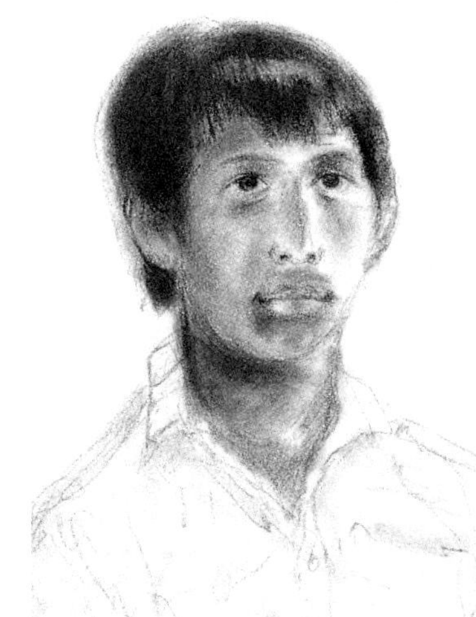

Above: I made this drawing of a ten-year-old Bangladeshi boy in conté crayon. He sat patiently for at least half an hour.

Right: this very rapid crayon drawing of a young boy, by James Mealing, was made while the boy was dozing off.

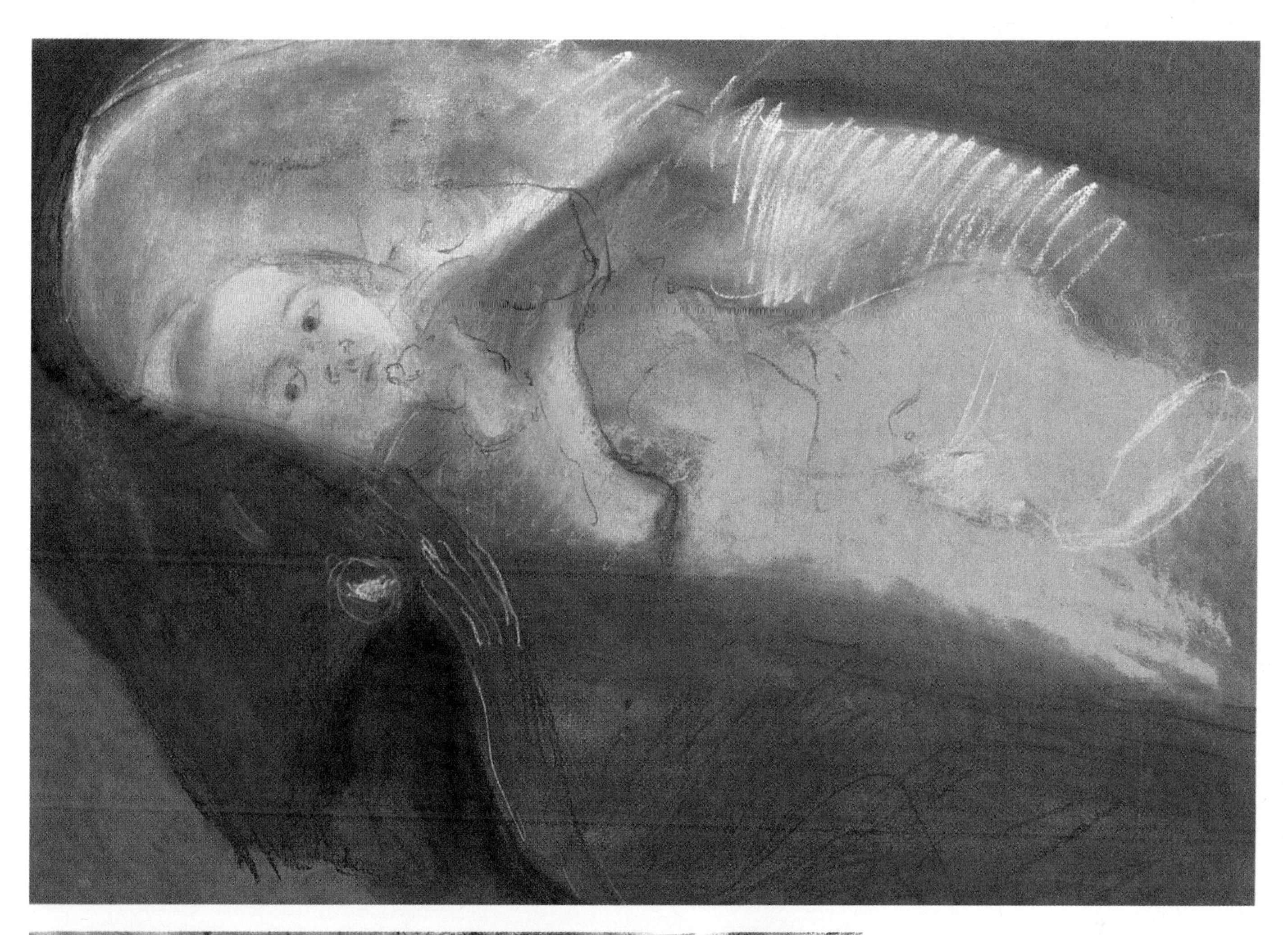

Above: this drawing of a young baby in his carry cot was made in one of those rare moments when a baby is actually awake, but still. I was lucky to be able to capture his very expressive eyes, which for me became the most important part of the drawing. It was done in pastel on brown Ingres/Strathmore paper.

Left: a pastel and conté drawing of three schoolgirls. I asked them to pose together for five minutes, so that I could put down the initial marks. Then they posed individually for ten minutes each while I developed the drawing. I added the school corridor in the background to give the drawing a sense of place.

MOTHER AND CHILD

I drew this picture in pastel directly onto the paper in front of the model and her small son. It was part of a series of drawings which I had to make at great speed, because the baby and mother moved constantly.

Right: these were the initial marks for a drawing I made of my sister and her child. Because I was using blue Ingres/Strathmore paper, I drew the marks in a colour that I knew would show up easily. I needed to get down the basic lines first as a guideline, to get a feeling of how the picture would fit together as a whole. At this point in a drawing I don't worry about detail.

Some of the drawings that I made of this mother and her child worked – others did not. I made over 20 in a three-day period. With this kind of speedy approach, one ultimately has to select the best and I selected ten.

Pastels were a good choice of media to use for these drawings, giving me fast coverage as well as a softness of line and colour that I felt appropriate to my subject.

I kept materials ready on a table that I could easily move and so follow the mother and baby to any location. This method requires fairly intense concentration – one becomes almost like a photographer waiting to capture the right moment.

Above: here I developed the colour in the picture. I had to work very quickly because my models were moving all the time. I laid in the basic colours rapidly, virtually losing the white marks underneath. At this stage I was trying almost to get rid of the blank paper and fill it with my image.

Above: my finished picture reflects the rapidity with which it was drawn and which gives it dynamism. In it I hope to have conveyed the moment of intimacy between the mother and her child.

DRAWING OLDER PEOPLE

Elderly people are a gift to draw. They have characterful faces and are often very patient with you, probably because many of them have more time to spare than other people. Remember, though, because of their age they can tire more easily than younger models.

One of the most noticeable characteristics of the ageing face is that the forehead is farther forward than the rest of the face, because the face is shrinking. (This is exactly the opposite to an infant's face, in which the forehead recedes.) This makes the shape of the skull more visible, and the hollows in the face more pronounced. The jawline tends to be less strong because of the loss of teeth. Curiously enough, the ears remain robust in comparison to the rest of the face and so seem larger than on older heads.

The shoulders of elderly people often slope, and their bodies shrink and tend to stoop. Their hands seem to take on much more importance as the bulk of the upper arms and shoulders disappears.

Observe the skin closely. Be careful not to draw the wrinkles and loose skin with arbitrary lines, otherwise they can look like ugly gashes.

Right: this charcoal portrait makes good use of the clothes to describe the form underneath. The loose marks of the charcoal convey the relaxed mood of the model.

Above: I made this drawing of my grandmother as she sat in her chair watching television. It was done in a mixture of graphite and pencil in a sketchbook.

Far right: During one of his trips to Nepal, Dan Williams made this drawing using conté crayon, applying the conté stick on its side in some places. The clothes become very large and important in this picture, making the figure inside them seem frail. This is a very penetrating portrait indeed.

USA

IN THE GYM

Gymnasiums of various kinds, whether for keep-fit, weightlifting or boxing, are excellent sources of reference for figure drawings. Quite simply, what you have is a room full of captive life models, all performing the kind of strenuous movements that a professional model would rarely agree to.

In a gym you can study plenty of fine physical specimens, who often repeat the same kind of movements, making drawing them relatively easy. You will also find that a lot of people who work out in these gyms are proud of their bodies and only too pleased to have the chance of posing for you!

I was virtually in residence at this particular gym for about a year and during this time I took hundreds of photographs and made even more fast sketches. These sketches were very small – gestural, pastel drawings. The larger, more ambitious compositions were made in the studio, such as the one developed here.

Above: I first scribbled out a basic idea of the composition for this image of a boxer in yellow and white pastel. Then, **right**, I worked into the paper with broader areas of colour. These areas filled in the basic forms and indicated the overall colour of the final piece, **far right**. By the end, I had worked into the drawing in great detail with pastel pencils and conté crayon, to give a finer line. This helped to mould and sculpt the broad areas of colour into solid and realistic looking forms.

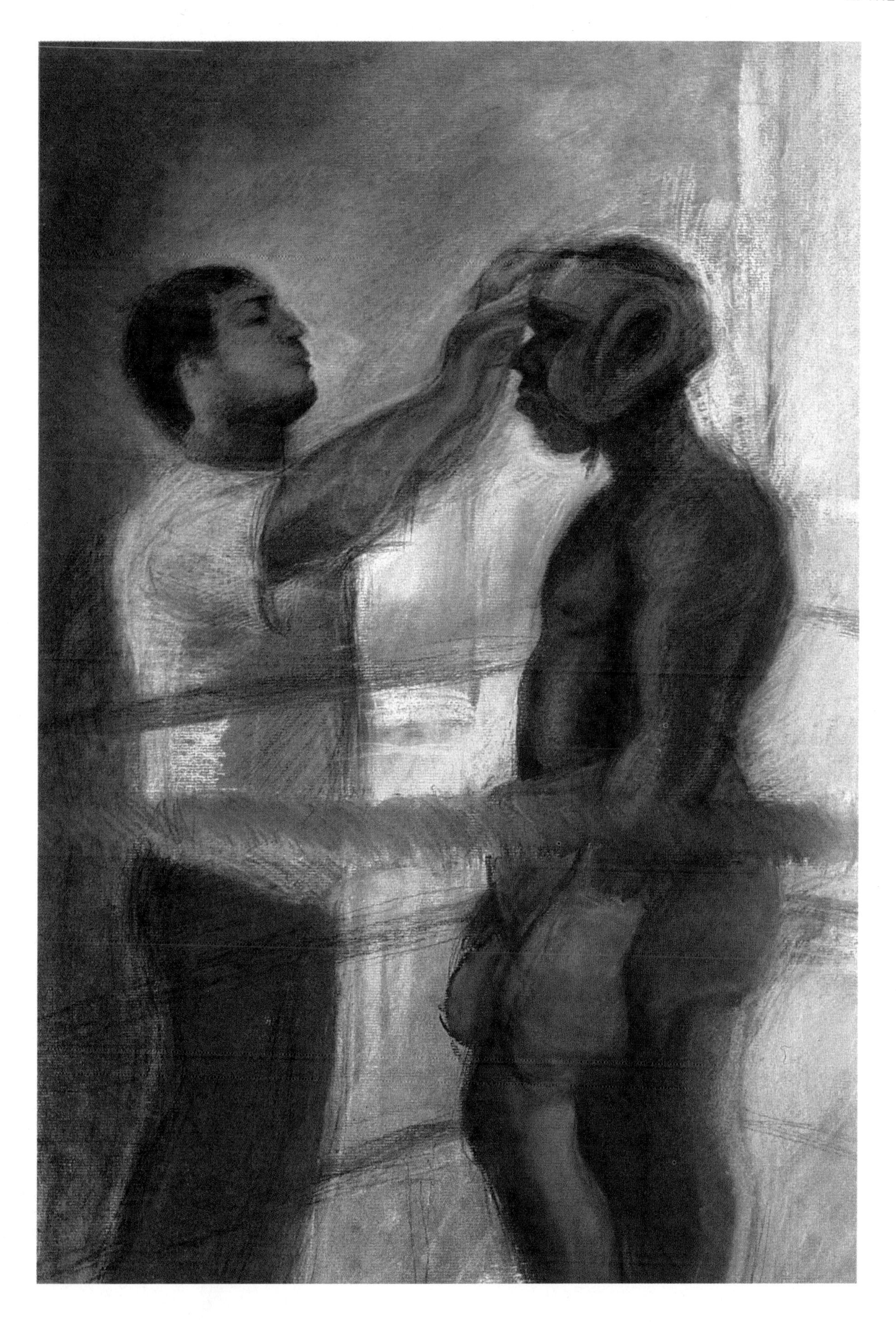

DANCERS AND MOVEMENT

Occasionally a dancer is invited to a life class or an opportunity to draw dancers in rehearsal arises. This provides the artist with the challenge of portraying the vitality, grace and beauty of the human body in motion.

Your first reaction, when trying to draw a dancer, may be sheer bewilderment and frustration as you try to fathom how to apply your careful study of anatomy, shape and form to a figure which is constantly moving. In fact, it is impossible, and the only answer is to simplify.

It is a good idea at first to look and try to feel the rhythm of the dancer's movements yourself. Then make quick gestures on the paper. You will achieve your own kind of shorthand this way.

You will find it easiest to use a direct and spontaneous medium, the kind you can smudge with your finger, such as conté, chalk or charcoal. You hardly need to look at your sheet of paper, but it is important to look at the model all the time. A dancer's hands and feet, for example, are very expressive and it is worth trying to get them right.

Get a series of drawings going in a spiralbound book so that you can constantly flick back and forth to work first on one drawing and then another, as the dancer's movements are repeated.

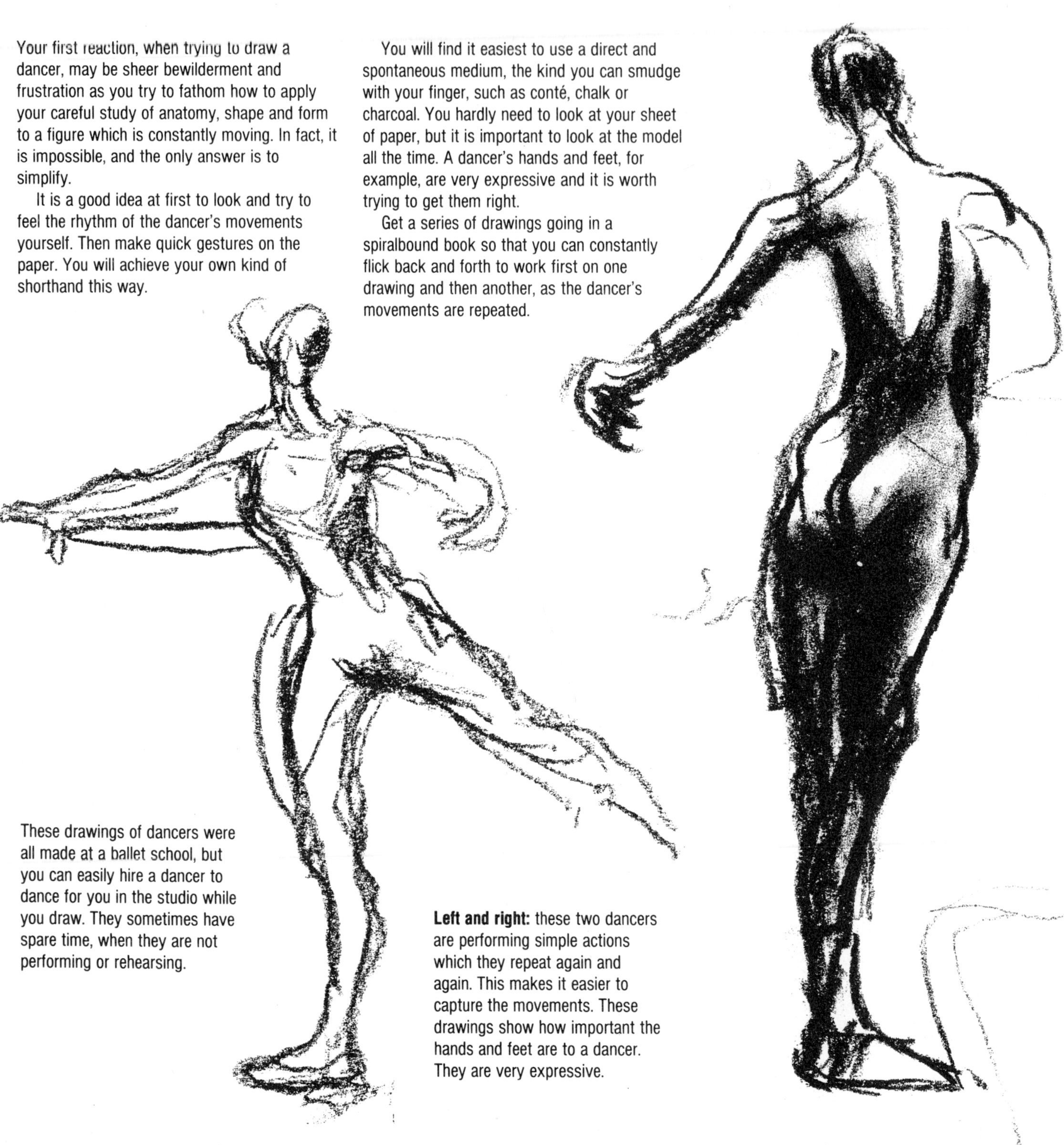

These drawings of dancers were all made at a ballet school, but you can easily hire a dancer to dance for you in the studio while you draw. They sometimes have spare time, when they are not performing or rehearsing.

Left and right: these two dancers are performing simple actions which they repeat again and again. This makes it easier to capture the movements. These drawings show how important the hands and feet are to a dancer. They are very expressive.

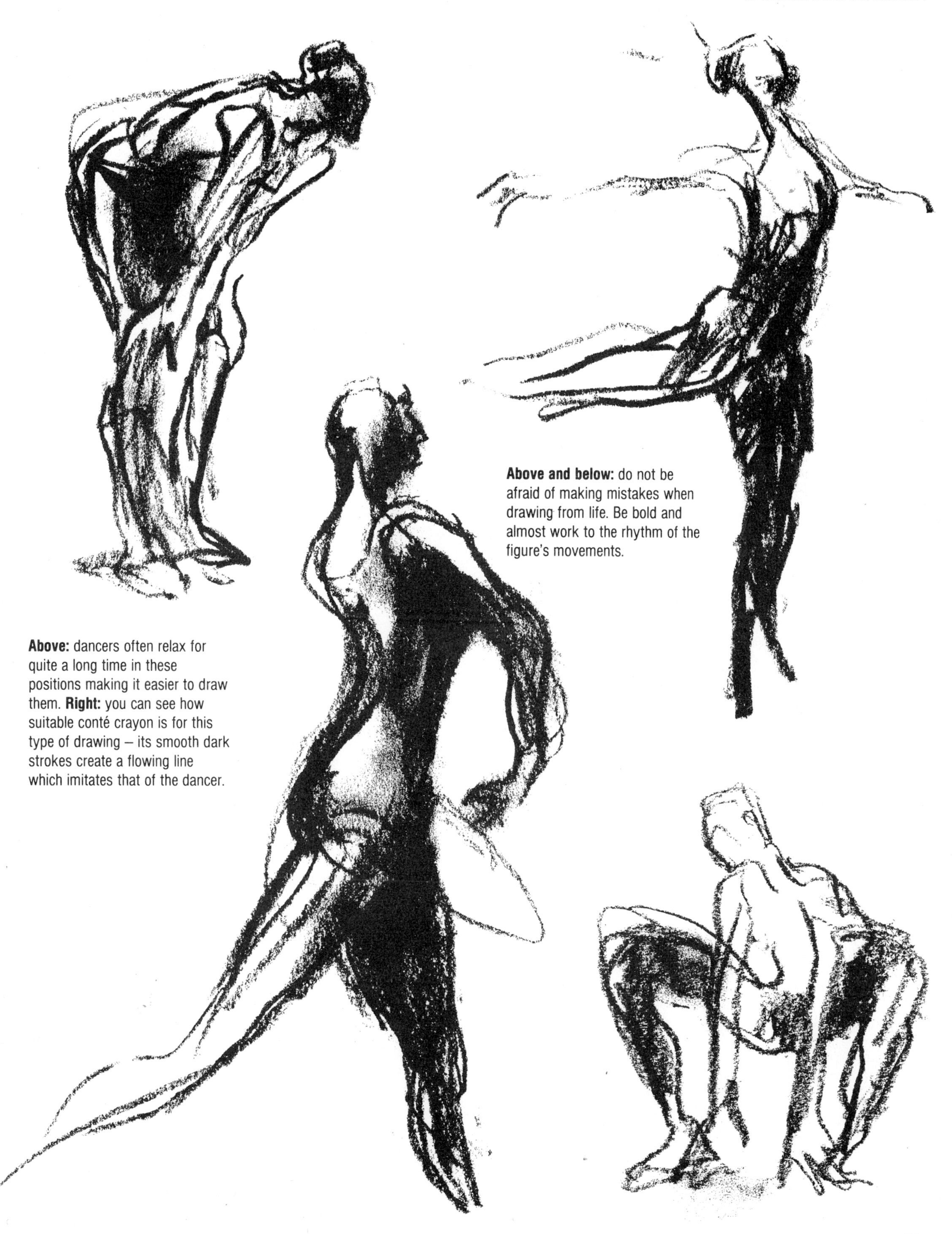

Above and below: do not be afraid of making mistakes when drawing from life. Be bold and almost work to the rhythm of the figure's movements.

Above: dancers often relax for quite a long time in these positions making it easier to draw them. **Right:** you can see how suitable conté crayon is for this type of drawing – its smooth dark strokes create a flowing line which imitates that of the dancer.

CLOTHING AND DRAPERY

Obviously, if we are to draw the people around us, we have to get accustomed to drawing the clothed figure. But drawing clothing and drapery can be a problem, especially when you have been used to drawing the nude figure. I have found that it helps to think of clothing as an essential part of the figure, rather than simply something that is laid on top of it.

Drapery used to be studied as a separate subject in art schools, and was somehow just added to the figure after it was drawn. Now, thankfully, it is considered to be part of the figure and is tackled in a more natural way.

It is a useful exercise to get a clothed model to pose in the life class. You will notice how the body affects the shape of the clothes if you observe it carefully. Clothes can also have a restricting effect on the movements of the body, and this is well illustrated in the drawings shown here.

Costumes can often be hired from local theatrical companies or shops, and are great fun to draw. They frequently change the model's character completely. You could even take the idea of costume further and draw people in uniform. I was once in a life class where a local fireman had been persuaded to sit for the class, complete with his axe, shiny helmet and boots.

You can always find uniformed people in their natural habitat for yourself. Police officers, waiters and waitresses, nurses, church ministers, soldiers, the mailman, and doormen in hotel lobbies are all transformed and given authority by their clothes. Studying uniformed people is a good exercise in studying the character that clothes lend a figure.

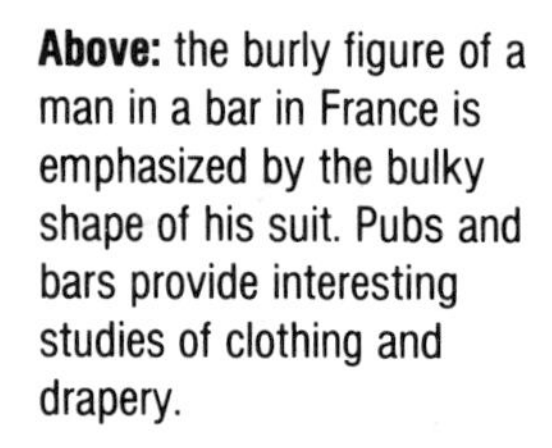

Above: the burly figure of a man in a bar in France is emphasized by the bulky shape of his suit. Pubs and bars provide interesting studies of clothing and drapery.

Left and right: these two drawings form part of a series which I made of myself getting dressed. Observing myself in a full-length mirror I then quickly drew what I had seen, in crayon. This is a good exercise in working speedily and teaches you to look at figures attentively.

Above and top: these lively costume drawings made in pencil resulted from hiring a theatrical costume for the studio model to wear.

Above and left: the character of the model is often transformed by a period costume and she will move and pose differently when wearing it.

Left and right: these are two more in the series of drawings I made of myself. Winter clothes are often restricting and tend to make the body alter its pose and movements. This is made very clear in an exercise such as this, which, traces the dressing sequence from nudity to being fully clothed.

ON LOCATION

Figure drawing can be done practically anywhere where there are people: the zoo, where the conjunction of people and animals is fascinating; the local park, where people picnicking, walking dogs, playing games, sailing boats or just sitting on benches provide ample models; a local market; circuses; dance halls; factories and building sites. The list is endless. Some of the possible locations are illustrated in the following section, with a discussion of the problems each situation presents.

An artist, more so than a photographer, is quite welcome in many places. But always be friendly and explain what you are doing. Let people know that the drawings are entirely for your own purposes, because sometimes they can be very suspicious. Another hazard of drawing in public, which you must prepare yourself for, is a sea of admiring faces behind you. However, a brief explanation will usually satisfy your audience and they will soon leave you in peace.

PREPARING TO WORK ON LOCATION

Careful preparation is essential if you are planning to work outdoors. The omission of one particular pencil from your kit can leave you with a wasted journey.

The first thing I decide on when getting ready for an open-air session is clothing. Will I be hot or too cold? It's a good idea to wear a hat in most weather conditions, either to keep you warm or to keep the sun off your head.

I find an old coat with plenty of pockets useful, and a spare jersey. It can always double up as a cushion if the weather is not cold.

A comfortable, collapsible stool is a useful item to carry with you. Fishing and camping accessory shops are worth a visit.

There is a wide variety of ingeniously designed portable easels, although I prefer a drawing board on my knees. I don't like to draw attention to myself, and the vagaries of English weather have put me off using an easel.

I always take a shoulder bag with me to carry equipment such as pencils, tissues, a craft knife, erasers, pastels and large clips, the last being absolutely essential for keeping all your drawings together.

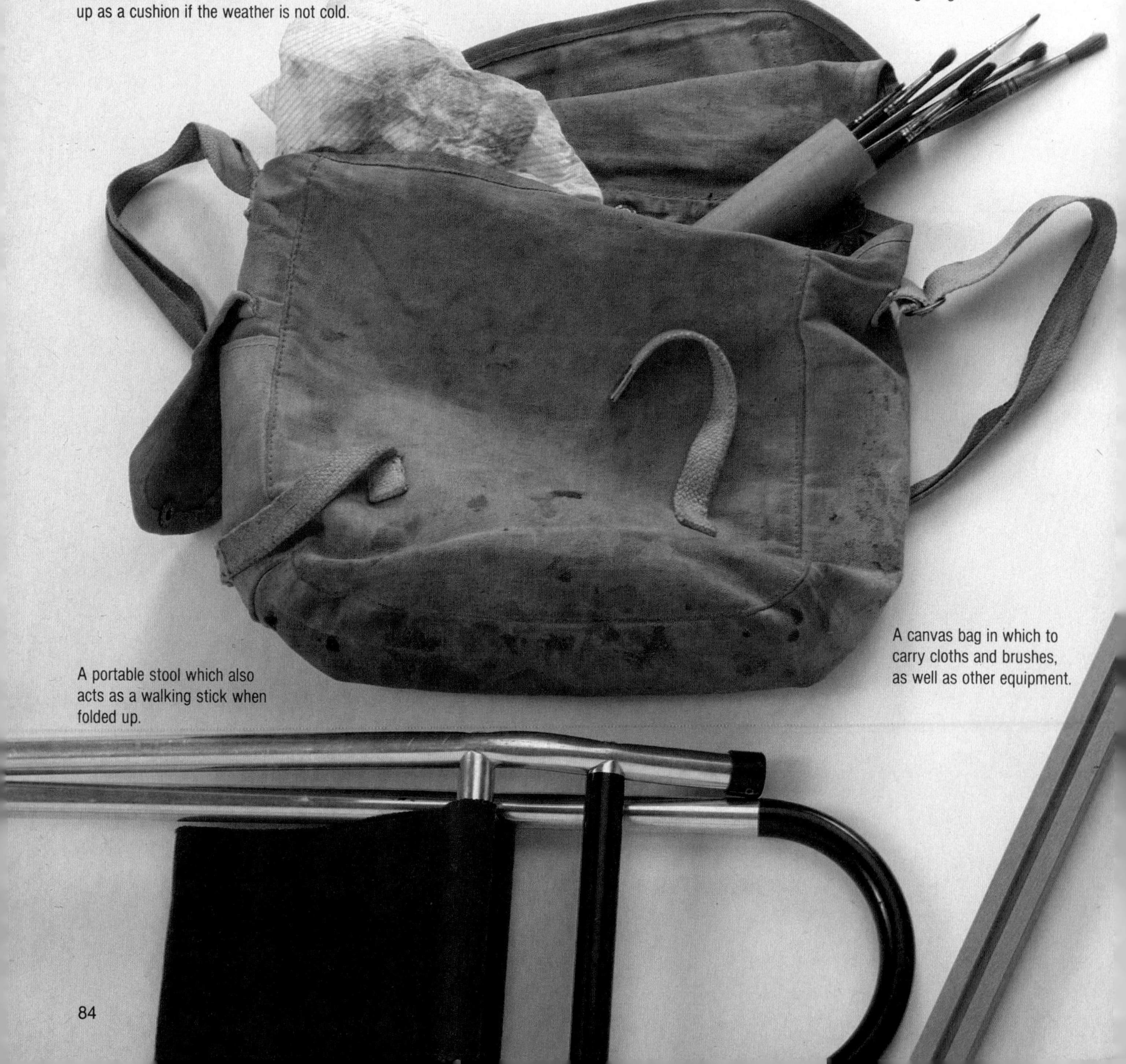

A canvas bag in which to carry cloths and brushes, as well as other equipment.

A portable stool which also acts as a walking stick when folded up.

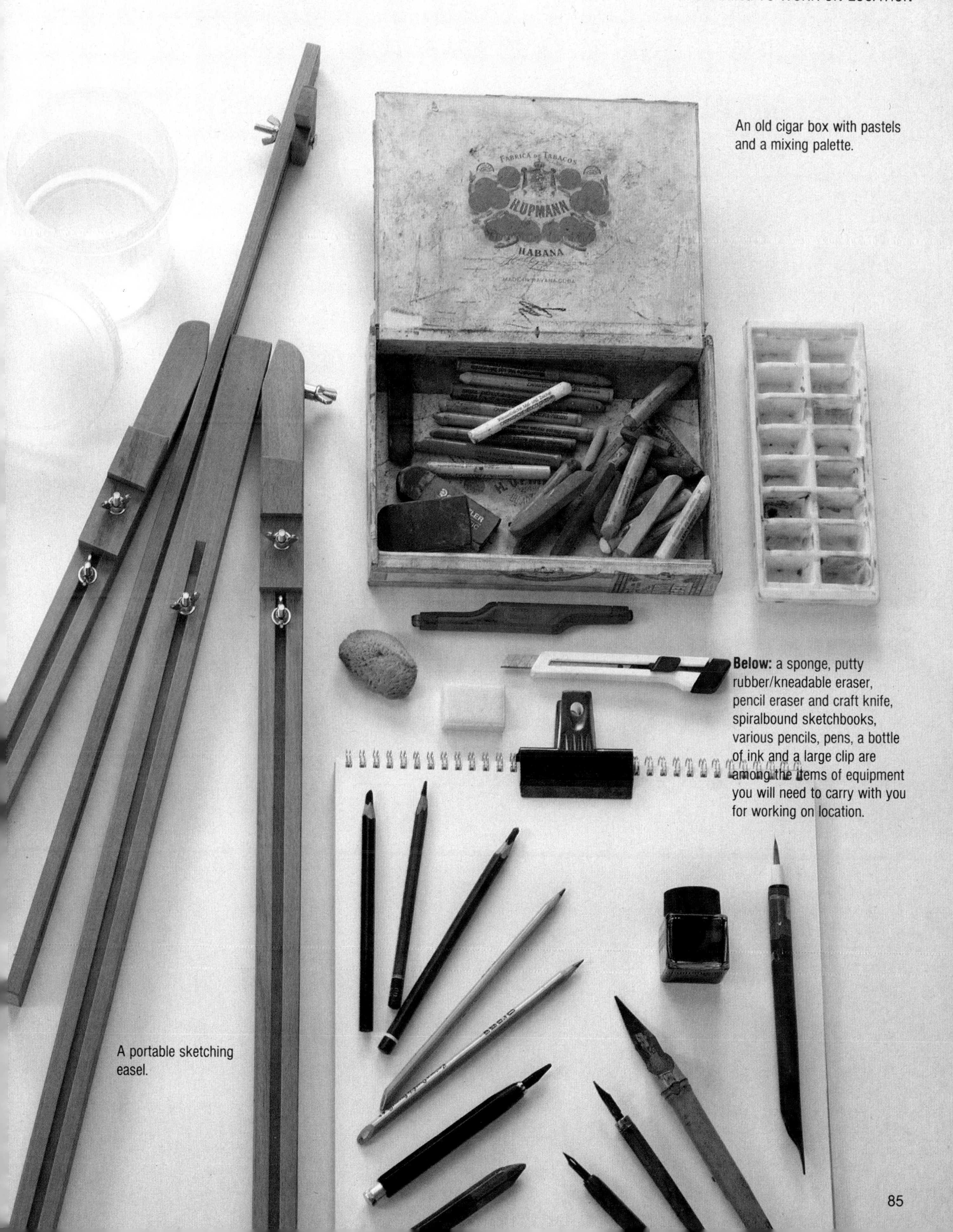

An old cigar box with pastels and a mixing palette.

Below: a sponge, putty rubber/kneadable eraser, pencil eraser and craft knife, spiralbound sketchbooks, various pencils, pens, a bottle of ink and a large clip are among the items of equipment you will need to carry with you for working on location.

A portable sketching easel.

THE SKETCHBOOK

An artist's sketchbook often contains the most spontaneous, lively and personal work that the artist ever does. Most artists, whether they are sculptors, designers or painters, carry a small sketchbook in their bag or pocket, sometimes to make ambitious drawings, sometimes just to make notes of colours or diagrams of compositions.

Always carry a sketchbook with you because you never know when you will want to make a drawing. It could be on the way to work or while you are out shopping.

A sketchbook is also extremely valuable when you are working on location: your drawings in it are automatically protected by the other pages and held together by the binding; in addition, a sketchbook with a sturdy cover dispenses with the need for carrying around a heavy drawing board.

You can make your own sketchbook very easily by simply sewing together sheets of paper. This way you get your own choice of paper, colours, textures and weights.

If you do not want to make a sketchbook, you will find a vast selection available from artists' suppliers, ranging from very large to pocket size. I generally use the spiralbound variety, because my sketches often turn out to be the finished thing, and I like to be able to tear them out easily.

Try not to work on the reverse side of a drawing because you will damage the first drawing.

Above: a very quick study in charcoal of what was probably a four-minute pose.

Right: a study from a spiralbound sketchbook of two different profiles. These kinds of sketches done on the spur of the moment keep your hand and eye attuned.

Right: during an orchestra rehearsal, the artist made this drawing in a sketchbook. Having only a limited amount of equipment, the artist was able to get quite close to the musicians.

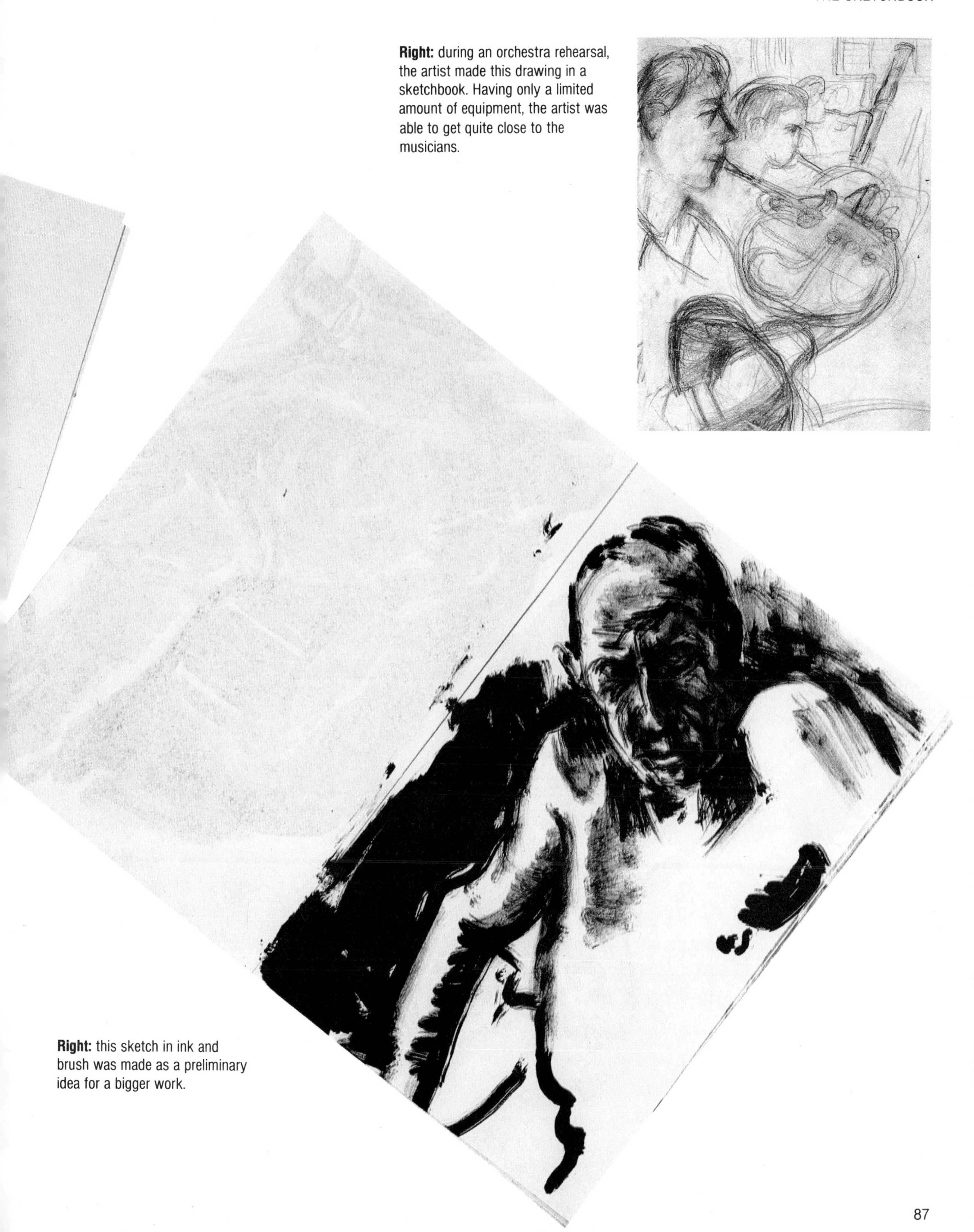

Right: this sketch in ink and brush was made as a preliminary idea for a bigger work.

Above: the second in a series of sketches of the orchestra, this is a more distant view of the whole ensemble, done in pencil.

Above: another drawing in the series of musicians. This sequence shows how the sketchbook can be used to build up several drawings of one particular subject, which could be referred to later for a more ambitious work, such as a painting.

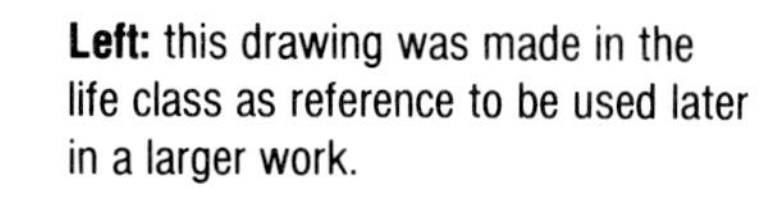

Left: this drawing was made in the life class as reference to be used later in a larger work.

Right: this final piece in the orchestral series is a very animated drawing of the conductor and the players in action.

Above: a detailed piece of work made in a very large sketchbook, in conté crayon.

DEALING WITH MOVEMENT

One of the first things that will undoubtedly frustrate and disconcert you when you venture out to draw people "on location" will be their constant movement. You cannot politely ask the truck driver you are drawing if he wouldn't mind keeping still! You will have to draw what you see and as it comes.

Some of the drawings here were done in the life class as practice for speed. The drawings of the choirmaster, however, were done at a gospel choir rehearsal.

Drawing movement requires a great deal of patience and practice. But remember, it is the spirit of the person you are drawing that is most important, and not necessarily anatomical accuracy, which can often get in the way of a really lively drawing.

You will find that people often repeat the same gesture or movement over and over again. So if you wait and watch, you will probably have another chance. By concentrating hard you will find that your drawings will be surprisingly accurate.

Do use a relatively simple and uncomplicated medium when drawing on location, because you won't have time to wait for a wash to dry, for example, or even to sharpen a pencil. So make sure that you are well prepared before you start.

Opposite far left: a lovely, simple drawing of the model stretching herself as she finished her pose.
Opposite left: the model pranced around the room in slow motion to make drawing her movements slightly easier. Note how the artist has not worried about dropping blobs of ink on the page – they do not detract at all from the drawing itself.
Above and above right: in these two drawings, the clothed model posed herself in attitudes of suspended animation. These studies were done with EE and EB pencils.
Right: this is the real thing! I captured this extremely excitable choirmaster of a gospel choir in pierre noir crayon and wash. I had to use rapid, almost calligraphic lines because his movements were so quick.

THE STREET

You don't have to go far to find subjects to draw – there are plenty in your local high street. Corners are good situations, or the junctions of roads. The bus queue, shoppers impossibly laden, motorcycle messengers, the street sweeper and people chatting on their doorsteps provide a wealth of "real" characters.

An artist drawing in the street is more vulnerable to the curiosity of passers-by than in most other locations, so be "streetwise".

I find that it is a good idea to lean against a wall so that people cannot stand behind me to watch me work (which can be most disconcerting). Do not take a lot of equipment because you may have to make a quick getaway – for a number of reasons. You will need to work pretty rapidly anyway, so don't use a medium which is fiddly and slow.

I often take photographs in conjunction with my drawings, so that I can add the backgrounds to my drawings later, when there is more time.

Below: punks are a common sight on the streets of London. They will often pose for you for a while because they are very proud of their appearance.

Above: this charcoal drawing puts figures into the context of the street, including the road, safety rails and a bus.

Left: orthodox Jews in Jerusalem going about their daily tasks. Even though these are sketches made on location, the individual drawings have been very carefully set out on the page.

Right: this street scene in Cairo is marvellously expressive of the chaotic atmosphere, where people become almost adjuncts to vehicles and street furniture such as statues, lights, kiosks and traffic signs.

SPORTING EVENTS

Sporting events are wonderful occasions for subject matter, because they are often feats of colour, and the figures of the athletes are often contorted into many strange and surprising shapes.

It is fascinating to watch the human body pushed to the limits of its capabilities and it can be very challenging to try to describe the figure harmonizing with mechanical equipment or horses. But these events can and do present problems for the artist.

The biggest problem you will face will probably be in capturing athletes moving at lightning speed. You may also find yourself so fascinated with what is going on around you that you forget about the drawing! One way to overcome these difficulties is to go as often as you can to one particular event so that you get used to it and become familiar with the movements of your subjects. You will then be able to decide exactly what it is you want to draw and concentrate on it.

It is obviously more difficult to go regularly to professional events, so I suggest that you attend those in which amateurs are taking part. An added advantage is that amateur sportsmen and women tend to be more relaxed about artists drawing them. To draw the pros, you usually have to write asking for their permission, and you could use this time in a better way.

Left: this drawing of a young boxer "shadow boxing" in the mirror was made very quickly, as is often necessary in these situations, in pastel on Ingres/Strathmore paper.
Above: a heavyweight boxer sparring, drawn in conté crayon. These drawings are both the result of many hours of observing boxers, and form part of a series which amounted, in the end, to perhaps sixty or seventy drawings.

Right: novice skiers are easier and more fun to draw than their more expert counterparts who move faster and take their sport more seriously. This series of drawings in crayon demonstrates that at least a vague indication of the equipment is absolutely essential for a subject such as this. Apart from the skis, the artist has concentrated on minimal details only, such as the bobble hats, which has made these drawings rather humorous and telling.

Below: the action of an athlete skipping is surprisingly stable, because the skipping is so fast that only the rope seems to move. Note how the pastel has been used in outline to suggest the colour of flesh on the arms, and the way the skipping rope is hinted at as a vague halo around the body.

MUSICIANS

Musicians are wonderful to draw because their movements and facial expressions are so expressive. I believe that if your drawings are good, you should be able to tell from them whether someone is playing Beethoven or Count Basie!

You can find musicians virtually anywhere and not just at concert halls – buskers in subways and shopping malls, school orchestras and amateur pop groups "jamming" in a garage all make interesting subjects.

You have the advantage over photographers at public performances because, whereas you can draw the musicians as much as you like, photography is frequently not allowed.

It doesn't matter if the lights are dimmed and you are drawing in the dark – if you have really looked hard at your subject, you will be amazed, when the lights go up, how lively the work is.

I especially love drawing in jazz clubs because the lighting tends to be so dramatic, the players have great character, the action is close-up and the atmosphere is intimate. Orchestras are usually very willing to let you draw them at rehearsals, although they like you to be absolutely silent, so scratching with hard pencils is out!

Opposite top: a pen and ink drawing of an army band playing in St James' Park, London. On the whole, this kind of scene has little movement in it, so it is possible to draw it with pen and ink, which is usually a fiddly medium that you can't change once you have applied it to the paper. The figures on deckchairs in the background all help to convey the atmosphere of a lazy summer's day.

Opposite left: a crayon drawing of jazz trombonist Al Grey, made at a club. I had to draw him very quickly, as he jumped around a lot in time to the music. You can see the faint lines where I had various false starts! Don't worry about these lines in your work – they can lend an appropriately hectic atmosphere to the drawing.

Opposite right: a violinist drawn in pencil. You can see how important it is to get the position of the instrument exactly right in relation to the body.

Left: this touching portrait of a Nepalese musician was made in conté crayon which was smudged with a rag in areas. The musician obviously posed for this drawing, which has been worked into in some detail. The hands are an extremely important element of any portrait of a musician, and have to bc drawn accurately.

PARKS

Parks are like huge theatres. Every imaginable kind of activity goes on in them, from children paddling in ponds, to bands playing in bandstands, from sports matches to courting couples, from elderly people soaking up the sun in deckchairs to joggers. There is always someone to draw in a park.

The backgrounds created by sky, grass and trees can throw up many interesting ideas for compositions, with perhaps more than one figure in them. There are usually plenty of places for you to sit and set up your gear, but beware of sitting in a quiet and lonely part. In my experience, there are occasionally some very unpleasant characters around in parks and it is better to be near people where you know you are safe. This will make you feel a lot more comfortable while you are working. This advice applies to all your locational visits, of course.

Right: this drawing, in pen and ink and watercolour wash, was done in the vast parklands of Versailles, where the statues often get mistaken for real people! The drawing took quite a long time to do.

Below: in contrast to the adjacent drawing, this was completed in a matter of minutes. It is a portrait of a businessman who regularly eats his lunch in the park.

Above: crowds of people enjoying a summer's day in St James' Park, London. The indication of the building in the background and the magnificent trees give the drawing a sense of place.

Above and right: you will find many people just sitting or standing around, taking the air, in a park. It's a good location for subjects to draw. The drawing above was done in crayon, and the one on the right is in brush and ink.

Above: this swift drawing is of a tourist taking a snapshot. The bag is an important detail in identifying him as a tourist.

THE MARKET

Markets are a great place to draw, because there are so many people around, so much hustle and bustle, and men and women going about a variety of tasks without any hint of self-consciousness.

Left: this sketch made on location served as the main reference for the final drawing opposite. I decided to use the figure in the foreground, but in a different context. The original sketch is more swiftly executed and less controlled than the final drawing, but since I knew it was for reference only, I worked in a very direct and gestural way.

Right: after blocking in the basic shapes of the composition I covered the paper with broad washes of pastel and then started to work into them with details, drawing on top of the washes. As I worked, I toned down the colour, because I found it too gaudy and unnatural. I also moved the figure in the foreground up a little. This shows just how flexible pastel can be if you do not make your marks too definite in the initial stages.

In this pastel drawing of Electric Avenue in South London, I have taken a figure from an original sketch made on location near the market. But I decided to change the background and put the figure into a slightly different context.

As you get more practised at figure drawing, you may want to try adding a background from another work to go with your figures. This is when you really start "picture making" rather than simply drawing.

Below: in the finished piece, here, the figure in the foreground fits in well with the new setting and makes a good contrast with the vague forms in the background. Conté crayon and white pastel were added to create highlights, particularly in the clouds and the electric light bulbs, and to intensify the yellow of the fruit on the stall, **left**. But I did not work any laborious detail into the drawing because this would have detracted from the energy of the original.

DRAWING FROM SCULPTURE

It may not have occurred to you that you can get figure drawing practice by drawing from sculpture. You can find some marvellous figures either in civic sculpture, on or in front of buildings or in parks, or in the permanent collections of museums.

Above: this monumental figure was drawn outside the Chaillot Palace in Paris. The very dark areas were realized by rubbing pierre noir crayon into the paper with tissue and drawing again on top of that. This is just a detail of the statue, which is actually enormous when seen close up. You get a sense of the solidity of the stone here, which contrasts with the liveliness of the Rodin figure on the left.

Left: I drew this maquette by Rodin in pen and ink in the Rodin museum in Paris. To create the shadow I smudged areas of ink with my finger. The model had an energy and passion which I wanted to convey in my drawing. It also gave me ideas for a possible pose in the life class.

One of the best reasons for drawing from sculptures is that the figures never move! It is also fascinating to see how the sculptor has dealt with form, volume and expression. I have learned many a valuable lesson from studying sculpture.

When dealing with sculpture, you are drawing a three-dimensional object that you can walk around. You can therefore choose a number of viewpoints and make up your own composition.

Do be aware of the material that the sculpture is made from. When drawing it, make it clear that it is a sculpture rather than a realistic figure. If you do try to make it look "real", the result will be strange and stiffly posed.

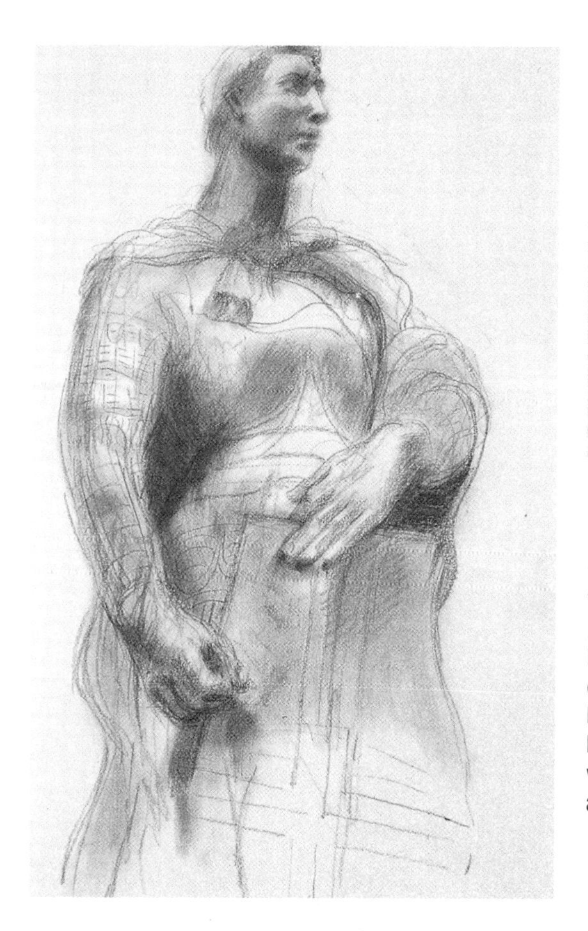

Left: in the Victoria and Albert Museum in London is a statue of St George, by Donatello. It was difficult to portray because of the very particular expression that the statue has – it is a slightly fierce and determined look which took me a long time to get right. I felt that the lightly clenched fist of his right hand was a significant part of the sculpture and had to be drawn with great care.

Above: these heads of two ladies were also in the Victoria and Albert Museum. I had no other equipment on that day except a biro pen, which, oddly, worked quite well in describing the detail of these carefully crafted faces. Certain passages of the drawing have been left fairly loose in order to focus attention on their beautiful profiles.

STORING AND DISPLAYING

As this book is about figure drawing, I will not go into great detail about picture framing. This is a big subject in itself and has been written about at length elsewhere. What I feel would be more helpful is to give advice about displaying and storing your work.

After your life drawing sessions, you will probably end up with lots of drawings, some successful, some not so successful. Many of them will not be worth framing, but you might still want to keep them. In this section you will find ideas and advice about looking after these pictures.

You need to be careful about fixing, storing and displaying your drawings because they can decay very quickly. If you take care of them, your drawings will give you and your friends many years of pleasure.

Daler
Daler
Daler

LOOKING AFTER YOUR DRAWINGS

At some time you will want to preserve some of your drawings. So here are a few tips on how to do this in a way that is not complicated or expensive.

If your drawings are done in charcoal, pastel, conté crayon or pencil, they must be carefully fixed. Spray them with a fixative, with the container held almost upright and with the spray nozzle at least 20cm (8in) away from the surface. It is better to use a mouth diffuser rather than an aerosol fixative.

Even after it has been fixed, a drawing is never completely protected. I like to cover all my drawings with a sheet of tissue or layout paper, because the medium always rubs off to some extent, particularly if the drawings are stored one on top of another, even if they are laid carefully in a drawer or plan chest.

The surest way to keep your work absolutely clean and flat is to put it into some kind of folder, such as an artist's portfolio or a photographer's bookleaf plastic file. The latter comes in smaller sizes than the portfolio. These folders will mean that your drawings are very easy to display without being ruined.

Framing, I believe, should be kept as simple as possible. What a good frame should do is lead the eye into the picture, not distract it with lots of embellishment. No amount of decoration or embellishment will make your drawing any better than it really is.

You can buy ready-made frames in the shops. Their main disadvantage is that they limit you to the manufacturers' sizes. Having your work framed professionally is probably the best answer because then you can choose a dimension and a frame moulding that will suit your picture. Also, especially if it is a pastel or charcoal drawing, you should take care that your picture is surrounded by an aperture mount/mat made of cardboard, which will keep the glass clear of the surface of your picture.

Two alternatives for framing are illustrated here. You can have a work framed professionally, as the larger work was done, in plain, unstained wood, with an aperture mount/mat; or you can frame your drawings in a ready-made clip frame that you assemble yourself.

When you store your work, you will need to protect it from damage by making sure it is kept clean and flat. Folders of different sizes are available for this purpose. A folio carrying case has a zip and a handle to transport work easily and safely. Artist's portfolios have sturdy covers and fasten with tape ties.

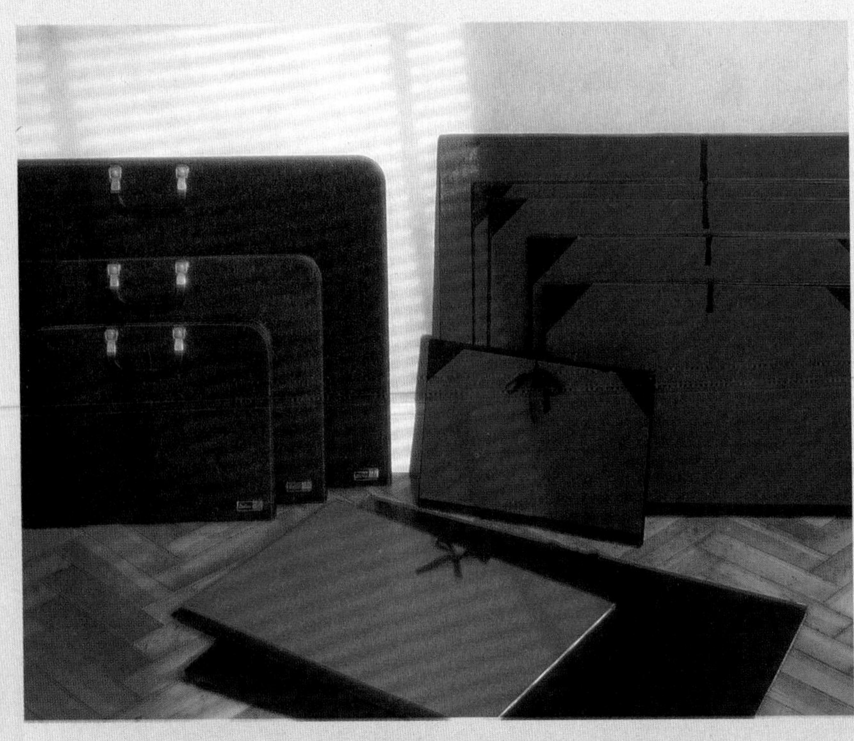

GLOSSARY

Antagonistic
A term which refers to muscles that work in opposition to each other. The triceps and biceps, for example, are antagonistic muscles; when the one contracts, the other relaxes.

Articulation
The flexibility or movement of the body about its joints.

Axes
The major horizontal lines of the body's shape; these include the lines between the shoulders, the waist, the hips, the knees and the ankles. When one axis tilts, it has a corresponding effect on at least one of the other axes, in order to balance the body.

Blending
A means of fusing, or achieving a subtle gradation between two colours. This can be done with a solvent, such as water or turpentine, by rubbing with a rag or sponge, a torchon or a finger, or by applying colour over the medium so that no join is visible.

Blocking in
Setting out the main areas or shapes of colour of an image, before detail is worked into it.

Cold Pressed
Also known as "Not", this refers to a medium-smooth paper which is not pressed through hot metal rollers when it is made.

Collage
A technique which involves creating an image from a variety of materials stuck onto a support. The word derives from the French verb *coller*, which means "to stick".

Composition
The aesthetic and balanced arrangement of shapes and colours in an image.

Crosshatching
A method of building up criss-crossed drawn lines to create tone. It is often used as a means of shading, to model shapes.

Fixing
Spraying a varnish onto a drawing to prevent it from fading and to protect the medium from being rubbed off.

Form
The shape of an object or person; it usually refers to a shape's three-dimensionality and is associated with volume.

Foreshortened
Refers to the distortion, or shortening, of perspective which results when an object or person lies along a near-horizontal or horizontal plane receding from the viewer.

Golden Section
A division of a line or rectangle so that the ratio of the smaller to the greater part is the same as that of the greater part to the whole. Its mathematical expression is 8:13, or 0.618:1. It is believed to be one of the most harmonious proportions and is often unconsciously applied in the composition of an image.

High-key
A term which refers to tones that are light and have little density. High-key tones result when an area of colour has light shining directly onto it.

Highlights
The most intensely illuminated points in an image; they are produced by leaving an area of the support blank or by applying white over the colour of the medium.

Hot Pressed
A term that describes a smooth-surfaced paper which is passed through hot metal rollers.

Medium
The material you use to draw or paint your image with, such as pencil, pastel, ink or watercolour.

Monoprint
Also known as monotype, this is a technique for making a print in which an image is painted onto a sheet of glass or metal and is then transferred to a sheet of paper. Alternatively, paint or ink can be applied to a sheet of paper, and a second sheet placed over that and drawn on, to pick up the medium on the reverse side.

Moulding
Drawing or painting an object or person with deliberate areas of light and shadow so that it takes on a three-dimensional form.

Mount/mat
The sheet of cardboard with a window cut into it that divides a framed work from the glass.

Painterly
The opposite of graphic, this term is used to describe a work which has no clear outlines and in which the colour is loosely applied.

Perspective
The depiction of depth and space on a flat surface. It can refer to linear perspective, which uses converging parallel lines to describe recession, or aerial perspective, which relies on increasingly lighter tones to indicate distance.

Pouncing
A method of transferring a drawing on paper to another support by pricking the outlines with a pin, placing the drawing over the surface to be painted, and stamping a sachet of charcoal along the pin pricks so that a dotted outline is left on the underlying support.

Resist
A technique of keeping areas free of colour, usually by applying a waterproof medium such as wax or oil pastel to the support. When a water-based medium such as ink or watercolour is applied over the resist, it colours only the areas where the resist has been left off.

Shade
To darken areas of a shape so that it seems to recede into space, and is given form. Also refers to the darker hue of a colour, usually made by adding black.

Spattering
Flicking paint onto the support either by drawing your thumb along the bristles of a brush dipped into a medium, or by shaking the brush over the support.

Square up
To draw a grid over an image so that it can be transferred accurately to a larger or smaller grid on another support. This is a means of scaling up or scaling down a drawing.

Stylize
To reduce a form to its basic shape; the opposite of realistic representation.

Support
The material on which your drawing or painting is made. It can be anything from paper to canvas, from fabric to a wall.

Tint
Usually refers to a lighter hue of a colour, made paler by the addition of white.

Tone
The density of an area of colour, from light to dark. Tones are described in degrees from light, mid to half tones, and dark tones.

Tooth
This term refers to the texture of paper. Rough or coarse-grained papers have more tooth than smooth papers.

Torchons
Twists of paper shaped like a thin pencil, used to blend pastel or soft pencil.

Viewpoint
The angle or position the artist takes up from which the model is studied.

Wash
A broad, uniform area of colour which often serves as a background. It usually refers to watercolour or ink, which is applied with a brush or sponge, but also describes areas of blended pastel.

INDEX

PICTURE CREDITS

All illustrations by Jane Stanton
except for the following:
Andrew Baker – p62, 63
Clare Buckle – Title page p60TL,
61TL, 64L, R, 65, 90BL, 92BL
Jenoe Barcsay – p13, 18L, R, 19, 20,
21, 22TL, B, TR, 24, 26B, 28BL
Ilsa Crapper – p33B
Bernadette Coxon – p8T, B, 37R, 46B,
46–47C, 47TR, 48R, 49TL, 69TL, 69B,
TR, 86L
C. M. Dixon – p8T, B
Peter Evans – p74R, 43BR, 44T, 68TL
The Burrell Collection – Glasgow
Museums and Art Galleries – p10B
Courtauld Institute Galleries – London
(Princes Gate Collection) – p11T
John Hutchinson – p16B, TL, TR, 17
Clare Jarrett – p30TL, TR, BL, 34TL,
TR, 35TL, B, 36TL, TR, BL, BR, 44BL,
BR, 45TL, 81TL, TR, BR, 88BL, 89BR,
96BR
Windsor Castle, Royal Library © 1988
"Her Majesty the Queen" – p9T
James Mealing – p70R, 87TR, 88TL,
TR, 89TR, 92TR
British Museum – p9B
Fitzwilliam Museum – p11BL, BR
Daler and Rowney – p5B, 14L, R, 56L,
58BL, 105, 106
Steve Tanner – p14–15, 39, 40–41, 42,
46–47, 48–49, 52–53, 84–85, 106–107
National Museum of Wales – p10T
Dan Williams – p33T, C, TR, B, 59TL,
75, 78–79, 80, 86B, 92BR, 93C, 95T, C,
BR, 98BL, 99BL, BC, BR

We would like to thank Windsor and
Newton for loaning their equipment.
The drawings of Jenoe Barcsay have
been reproduced by courtesy of his
successor.